World's Funniest and Greatest E-mails

Compiled by R. Milligan and Will Stark

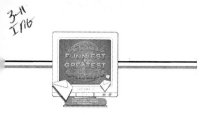

Published by IDT 3400 Ben Lomond Place, Suite 129, Hollywood Hills, CA 90027
www.IDT-us.com
Printed in the United States of America

Compiled by R. Milligan and Will Stark
Cover Design by Jeff Indusi
Interior Design by The Printed Page

ISBN: 0-9749720-0-2

This book is dedicated to Ron Milligan and Jeff Induci that were involved in the production of this book.

They left us this year and we miss them both, very much.

Contents

World's Funniest and Greatest E-mails

exciting!
emotional!

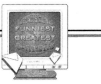

Chapter 1

Gender Humor

World's Funniest and Greatest E-mails

A young couple on their wedding night were in their honeymoon suite.

As they were undressing for bed, the husband, a big burly man, tossed his trousers to his new bride. He said, "Here, put these on."

She put them on and the waist was twice the size of her body.

"I can't wear your trousers." she said.

"That's right," said the husband, "and don't you ever forget it. I'm the man who wears the pants in this family."

With that she flipped him her panties and said, "Try these on."

He tried them on and found he could only get them on as far as his kneecaps.

"Hell," he said. "I can't get into your panties!"

She replied, "That's right...and that's the way it is going to stay until your attitude changes."

❊❊❊

Two times a week we go to a nice restaurant, have a little beverage, then comes good food and companionship. She goes on Tuesdays, I go on Fridays.

We also sleep in seperate beds. Her's is in Ontario and mine in Tucson.

I take my wife everywhere, but she keeps finding her way back.

I asked my wife where she wanted to go for our anniversary. "Somewhere I haven't been in a long time," she said. So I suggested the kitchen.

We always hold hands. If I let go she shops.

She has an electric blender, electric toaster and an electric bread maker. Then she said, "There are too many gadgets and no place to sit down." So I bought her an electric chair.

2

I married Miss Right. I just didn't know her first name was Always.

My wife told me the car wasn't running well because there was water in the carburetor. I asked her where the car was, she told me, "In the Lake."

She got a mudpack and looked great for two days. Then the mud fell off.

Statistcally, 100 percent of all divorces start with marriage.

She ran after the garbage truck yelling "Am I too late for the garbage?" The driver said, "No, jump in."

I haven't spoken to my wife in eighteen months. I don't like to interrupt her.

The last fight was my fault. My wife asked "What's on the TV?" I said, "Dust!"

❀❀❀

Subject: Mary and Jim

Jim and Mary were both patients in a mental hospital.

One day while they were walking past the hospital swimming pool, Jim suddenly jumped into the deep end. He sank to the bottom and stayed there. Mary promptly jumped in to save him. She swam to the bottom and pulled Jim out.

When the medical director became aware of Mary's heroic act he immediately ordered her to be discharged from the hospital, as he now considered her to be mentally stable.

When he went to tell Mary the news he said, "Mary, I have good news and bad news. The good news is you're being discharged because since you were able to jump in and save the life of another patient, I think you've regained your senses.

Entertaining!
Amazing!

The bad news is, Jim, the patient you saved, hung himself with his bathrobe belt in the bathroom. I am so sorry, but he's dead."

Mary replied "He didn't hang himself, I put him there to dry."

❋❋❋

I think this is why lawyers always tell their clients not to say anything.

WOMAN: What would you do if I died? Would you get married again?
MAN: Definitely not!
WOMAN: Why not — don't you like being married?
MAN: Of course I do.
WOMAN: Then why wouldn't you remarry?
MAN: Okay, I'd get married again.
WOMAN: You would? (with a hurtful look on her face)
MAN: (makes audible groan)
WOMAN: Would you sleep with her in our bed?
MAN: Where else would we sleep?
WOMAN: Would you replace my pictures with hers?
MAN: That would seem like the proper thing to do.
WOMAN: Would she use my golf clubs?
MAN: No, she's left-handed.
WOMAN: —- silence —
MAN: Shit!.

❋❋❋

Exciting!
Emotional!

A couple shopping at Wal-Mart got separated. The man walks up to an attractive woman and tells her that he has lost his wife in the store.

The woman looks him up and down then asks, "Why are you telling me about it?" His response, "Every time I talk to an attractive gal with big boobs, she shows up."

※※※

A man and woman are at a bar having a few beers. They start talking and soon realize they're both doctors. After an hour, the man says, "Hey, how about if we sleep together tonight? No strings attached." The woman doctor agrees to it. They go back to her place and he goes in the bedroom. She goes into the bathroom and starts scrubbing up like she's about to go into the operating room. She scrubs for a good 10 minutes. At last, she goes into the bedroom and they have sex.

Afterward, the man says, "You're a surgeon, aren't you?" "Yes," says the woman, "how did you know?" "I could tell by the way you scrubbed up before we started," he says. "That makes sense," says the woman. "You're an anaesthesiologist, aren't you?" "Yeah, how did you know?" asks the man. The woman replies, "Because I didn't feel a thing."

※※※

Just a reminder of how clever the female population can be!

There was a man who had worked all of his life and had saved all of his money. He was a real miser when it came to his money. He loved money more than just about anything, and just before he died, he said to his wife, "Now listen, when I die, I want you to take all my money and place it in the casket with me. I wanna take my money to the afterlife."

Entertaining!
Amazing!

So he got his wife to promise him with all her heart that when he died, she would put all the money in the casket with him.

Well, one day he died. He was stretched out in the casket, the wife was sitting there in black next to her closest friend. When they finished the ceremony, just before the undertakers got ready to close the casket, the wife said "Wait just a minute!" She had a shoe box with her, she came over with the box and placed it in the casket. Then the undertakers locked the casket down and rolled it away. Her friend said, "I hope you weren't crazy enough to put all that money in the casket."

She said, "Yes, I promised. I'm a good Christian, I can't lie. I promised him that I was going to put that money in that casket with him."

"You mean to tell me you put every cent of his money in the casket with him?"

"I sure did," said the wife. "I got it all together, put it into my account and I wrote him a check."

Send this to every "Clever Female" you know!

☀☀☀

An E-mail to the Wrong Wife

After being nearly snowbound for two weeks last winter, a Seattle man departed for his vacation in Miami Beach, where he was to meet his wife the next day at the conclusion of her business trip to Minneapolis. They were looking forward to pleasant weather and a nice time together. Unfortunately, there was some sort of mix-up at the boarding gate, and the man was told he would have to wait for a later flight. He tried to appeal to a supervisor but was told the airline was not responsible for the problem and it would do no good to complain.

@xciting!
@motional!

Upon arrival at the hotel the next day, he discovered that Miami Beach was having a heat wave, and its weather was almost as uncomfortably hot as Seattle's was cold. The desk clerk gave him a message that his wife would arrive as planned.

He could hardly wait to get to the pool area to cool off, and quickly sent his wife an e-mail, but due to his haste, he made an error in the e-mail address. His message therefore arrived at the home of an elderly preacher's wife whose even older husband had died only the day before!

When the grieving widow opened her e-mail, she took one look at the monitor, let out an anguished scream, and fell to the floor dead. Her family rushed to her room where they saw this message on the screen: "Dearest wife, Departed yesterday as you know. Just now got checked in. Some confusion at the gate. Appeal was denied. Received confirmation of your arrival tomorrow. Your loving husband. P.S. Things are not as we thought. You're going to be surprised at how hot it is down here."

❋❋❋

A woman meets a gorgeous man in a bar. They talk, they connect, they end up leaving together. They go back to his place, and as he shows her around his apartment, she notices that his bedroom is completely packed with sweet cuddly teddy bears.

Hundreds of cute small bears on a shelf all the way along the floor. Cuddly medium-sized ones on a shelf a little higher. Huge enormous bears on the top shelf along the wall.

The woman is surprised that this guy would have a collection of teddy bears, especially one that's so extensive, but she decides not to mention this to him, and actually is quite impressed by this evidence of his sensitive side! She turns to him,

Entertaining!
Amazing!

invitingly…they kiss…and then they rip each other's clothes off and make hot steamy love.

After she has this intense night of passion with this sensitive guy, and they are lying there together in the afterglow, the woman rolls over and asks, smiling, "Well, how was it for you?"

The guy yawns: "Help yourself to any prize from the bottom shelf."

※ ※ ※

A newlywed couple had only been married for two weeks. The husband, although very much in love, couldn't wait to go out on the town and party with his old buddies. So, he said to his new wife, "Honey, I'll be right back…"

"Where are you going, coochy cooh…?" asked the wife.

"I'm going to the bar, pretty face. I'm going to have a beer."

The wife said, "You want a beer, my love?" She opened the door to the refrigerator and showed him 25 different kinds of beer, brands from 12 different countries: Germany, Holland, Japan, India, etc.

The husband didn't know what to do, and the only thing that he could think of saying was, "Yes, loolie loolie…but at the bar…you know…they have frozen glasses…"

He didn't get to finish the sentence, because the wife interrupted him by saying "You want a frozen glass, puppy face?" She took a huge beer mug out of the freezer, so frozen that she was getting chills just holding it.

The husband, looking a bit pale, said, "Yes, tootsie roll, but at the bar they have those hors d'oeuvres that are really delicious…I won't be long. I'll be right back. I promise. OK?"

8

Exciting!
Emotional!

"You want hors d'oeuvres, poochi pooh?" She opened the oven and took out 15 dishes of different hors d'oeuvres: chicken wings, pigs in a blanket, mushroom caps, pork strips, etc.

"But sweet honey...at the bar...you know...there's swearing, dirty words and all that..."

"You want dirty words, cutie pie?...

LISTEN, DICKHEAD! DRINK YOUR FUCKING BEER IN YOUR GOD-DAMN FROZEN MUG AND EAT YOUR MOTHERFUCKING SNACKS, BECAUSE YOU AREN'T GOING ANYWHERE! GOT IT, ASSHOLE?"

☀☀☀

A wealthy man was having an affair with an Italian woman for several years.

One night, during one of their rendezvous, she confided in him that she was pregnant.

Not wanting to ruin his reputation or his marriage, he paid her a large sum of money if she would go to Italy to secretly have the child.

If she stayed in Italy to raise the child, he would also provide child support until the child turned 18.

She agreed, but asked how he would know when the baby was born.

To keep it discreet, he told her to simply mail him a post card, and write "Spaghetti" on the back.

He would then arrange for child support payments to begin.

One day, about 9 months later, he came home to his confused wife.

"Honey," she said, "you received a very strange post card today."

"Oh, just give it to me and I'll explain it later," he said.

9

Entertaining!
Emazing!

The wife obeyed, and watched as her husband read the card, turned white, and fainted.

On the card was written: "Spaghetti, Spaghetti, Spaghetti. Two with meat-balls, one without."

☀☀☀

A couple was invited to a swanky masked Halloween party. She got a terrible headache and told her husband to go to the party alone. He, being the devoted husband, protested, but she argued and said she was going to take some aspirin and go to bed and there was no need of his good time being spoiled not going.

So, he took his costume and away he went. The wife, after sleeping soundly for one hour, awakened without pain and, since it was still early, she decided to go to the party. Since her husband did not know what her costume was, she thought she would have some fun by watching her husband to see how he acted when she was not with him.

She joined the party and soon spotted her husband cavorting around on the dance floor, dancing with every nice chick he could and copping a little feel here and a little kiss there. His wife sidled up to him and, being a rather seductive lady herself, he left his partner high and dry and devoted his time to the new stuff that had just arrived. She let him go as far as he wished, naturally, since he was her husband. Finally, he whispered a little proposition in her ear and she agreed, so off they went to one of the cars and had sex.

Just before unmasking at midnight she slipped away and went home and put the costume away and got into bed, wondering what kind of explanation he would make for his behavior.

Exciting! Emotional!

She was sitting up reading when he came in and asked him what kind of time he had. He said, "Oh, the same old thing. You know I never have a good time when you're not there." Then she asked, "Did you dance much?"

He replied, "I'll tell you, I never even danced one dance. When I got there I met Pete, Bill Brown and some other guys, so we went into the den and played poker all evening...but you're not gonna believe what happened to the guy I loaned my costume to."

✸✸✸

One night a guy takes his girlfriend home. As they are about to kiss each other goodnight at the front door, when the guy starts feeling a little horny.

With an air of confidence, he leans with his hand against the wall and smiling, he says to her, "Honey, would you give me a blow job?"

Horrified, she replies, "Are you mad? My parents will see us!"

"Oh, come on! Who's gonna see us at this hour?" He asks grinning at her.

"No, please. Can you imagine if we get caught?"

"Oh, come on! There's nobody around, they're all sleeping!"

"No way. It's just too risky!"

"Oh, please, please, I love you so much!"

"No, no, and no. I love you too, but I just can't!"

"Oh, yes you can. Please?"

"No, no. I just can't"

"I'm begging you..."

Out of the blue, the light on the stairs goes on, and the girl's sister shows up in her pajamas, hair disheveled, and in a sleepy voice she says, "Dad says to go ahead and give him a blow job, or I can do it. Or if need be, Mom says she can come down herself and do it. But for God's sake tell him to take his hand off the intercom!"

Entertaining!
Amazing!

☀ ☀ ☀

1 – Her Diary

Saturday night I thought he was acting weird. We had made plans to meet at a bar to have a drink. I was shopping with my friends all day long, so I thought he was upset at the fact that I was a bit late, but he made no comment.

Conversation wasn't flowing so I suggested that we go somewhere quiet so we could talk, he agreed but he kept quiet and absent.

I asked him what was wrong he said nothing. I asked him if it was my fault that he was upset. He said it had nothing to do with me and not to worry.

On the way home I told him that I loved him, he simply smiled and kept driving. I can't explain his behavior; I don't know why he didn't say "I love you, too."

When we got home I felt as if I had lost him, as if he wanted nothing to do with me anymore. He just sat there and watched television. He seemed distant and absent.

Finally I decided to go to bed, about 10 minutes later he came to bed and to my surprise he responded to my caress and we made love, but I still felt that he was distracted and his thoughts were somewhere else. I decided that I could not take it anymore so I decided to confront him with the situation but he had fallen asleep. I started crying and cried until I too fell asleep. I don't know what to do. I'm almost sure that his thoughts are with someone else. My life is a disaster.

2 – His Diary

Today the Raiders lost.
At least I got laid.

☀ ☀ ☀

Exciting!
Emotional!

Jake was on his deathbed. His wife Susan was maintaining a vigil by his side. She held his fragile hand, tears running down her face. Her praying roused him from his slumber. He looked up and his pale lips began to move slightly. "My darling Susan," he whispered.

"Hush, my love," she said: "rest, don't talk."

"Susan," he said in his tired voice. "I have something I must confess to you."

"There' nothing to confess," replied the weeping Susan. "Everything is all right, go to sleep."

"No no. I must die in peace, Susan. I slept with your sister, your best friend and your mother."

"I know," she replied. "That's why I poisoned you."

✹✹✹

Young King Arthur was ambushed and imprisoned by the monarch of a neighboring kingdom. The monarch could have killed him, but was moved by Arthur's youth and ideals.

So the monarch offered him freedom as long as he could answer a very difficult question. Arthur would have a year to figure out the answer. If, after a year, he still had no answer, he would be put to death...

The question: What do women really want?

Such a question would perplex even the most knowledgeable man, and, to young Arthur, it seemed an impossible query. But, since it was better than death, he accepted the monarch's proposition to have an answer by year's end.

He returned to his kingdom and began to poll everybody: the princess, the prostitutes, the priests, the wise men and the court jester. He spoke with everyone, but no one could give him a satisfactory answer.

13

Entertaining!
Amazing!

Many people advised him to consult the old witch. Only she would know the answer. The price would be high; the witch was famous throughout the kingdom for the exorbitant prices she charged.

The last day of the year arrived and Arthur had no alternative but to talk to the witch. She agreed to answer the question, but he'd have to accept her price first: The old witch wanted to marry him.

Young Arthur was horrified: She was hunchbacked and hideous, had only one tooth, smelled like sewage and made obscene noises. He had never encountered such a repugnant creature.

Finally, having no real choice, he agreed. Their wedding was proclaimed, and the witch answered Arthur's question thus: What a woman really wants is to be in charge of her own life. Everyone instantly knew that the witch had uttered a great truth and that Arthur's life would be spared. And so it was. The neighboring monarch granted Arthur total freedom.

What a wedding Arthur and the witch had! Arthur was torn between relief and anguish. He was proper as always, gentle and courteous. The old witch put her worst manners on display, and generally made everyone very uncomfortable.

The hour approached. Arthur, preparing himself for a horrific experience, entered the bedroom. But what a sight awaited him! The most beautiful woman he'd ever seen lay before him! The astounded Arthur asked what had happened. The beauty replied that since he had been so kind to her when she'd appeared as a witch, she would henceforth be her horrible, deformed self half the time, and the other half she would be her beautiful maiden self.

Which would he want her to be during the day, and which during the night?

What a cruel question! Arthur pondered his predicament. During the day, a beautiful woman to show off to his friends, but at night, in the privacy of his home,

14

Exciting!
Emotional!

an old witch? Or would he prefer having by day a hideous witch, but by night a beautiful woman with whom to enjoy many intimate moments?

What would you do?

What Arthur chose follows below…but don't read until you've made your own choice…

Noble Arthur replied that he would let her choose for herself.

Upon hearing this, she announced that she would be beautiful all the time, because he had respected her enough to let her be in charge of her own life.

What is the moral of this story?

The moral is: If your woman doesn't get her own way, things are going to get ugly!

❋ ❋ ❋

A little good-natured male bashing…All in fun of course…

Q – What should you do when you see ex-husband rolling around in pain on the ground?

A – Shoot him again.

Q – Why do little boys whine?

A – They're practicing to be men.

Q – How many men does it take to screw in a light bulb?

A – One – he just holds it up there and waits for the world to revolve around him.

Or Alternate answer – Three: one to screw in the bulb and two to listen to him brag about the screwing part.

Entertaining!
Amazing!

Q – What do you call a handcuffed man?
A – Trustworthy.

Q – What does it mean when a man is in your bed gasping for breath and calling your name?
A – You didn't hold the pillow down long enough.

Q – Why does it take 100,000,000 sperm to fertilize one egg?
A – Because not one will stop and ask for directions.

Q – What's the best way to kill a man?
A – Put a six-pack and a naked woman in front of him and ask him to choose just one.

Q – What do men and pantyhose have in common?
A – They either cling, run or don't fit right in the crotch.

Q – Why do men whistle while they're on the toilet?
A – Because it helps them remember which end they need to wipe.

Q – What is the difference between men and women?
A – A woman wants one man to satisfy her every need. A man wants every woman to satisfy his one need.

Q – How does a man keep his youth?
A – By giving her money, diamonds and furs.

Q – How do you keep your husband from reading your e-mail?
A – Rename the mail folder to "instruction manuals."

Feel free to send this to five bright, funny women you know to make their day. At least finding five bright, funny women is possible!

❀❀❀

1. A couple is lying in bed. The man says, "I am going to make you the happiest woman in the world." The woman says, "I'll miss you."

2. "It's just too hot to wear clothes today," Jack says as he stepped out of the shower, "honey, what do you think the neighbors would think if I mowed the lawn like this?"
   "Probably that I married you for your money," she replied.

3. He said – "Shall we try swapping positions tonight?" She said – "That's a good idea…you stand by the ironing board while I sit on the sofa and fart."

4. He said – "What have you been doing with all the grocery money I gave you?" She said – "Turn sideways and look in the mirror."

5. Q: What do you call an intelligent, good looking, sensitive man?
   A: A rumor

6. One day my housework-challenged husband decided to wash his sweatshirt. Seconds after he stepped into the laundry room, he shouted to me, "What setting do I use on the washing machine?"
   "It depends," she replied. "What does it say on your shirt?"
   He yelled back, "University of Oklahoma."

And they say blondes are dumb…

❀❀❀

Entertaining!
Amazing!

It has been known for many years that sex was good exercise, but until now nobody had made a scientific study of the caloric content of different sexual activities. Now after "original and proprietary" research they are proud to present, to the LOVE group, the results.

REMOVING HER CLOTHES:
With her consent .... 12 Calories
Without her consent .... 2187 Calories

OPENING HER BRA:
With both hands .... 8 Calories
With one hand .... 12 Calories
With your teeth .... 485 Calories

PUTTING ON A CONDOM:
With an erection .... 6 Calories
Without an erection .... 3315 Calories

POSITIONS:
Missionary .... 12 Calories
69 lying down .... 78 Calories
69 standing up .... 812 Calories
Wheelbarrow .... 216 Calories
Doggy Style .... 326 Calories
Italian chandelier .... 2912 Calories

ORGASMS:
Real .... 112 Calories
Fake .... 1315 Calories

Exciting!
Emotional!

POST ORGASM:
Lying in bed hugging .... 18 Calories
Getting up immediately .... 36 Calories
Explaining why you got out of bed immediately .... 816 Calories

GETTING A SECOND ERECTION: If you are:
20–29 years .... 36 Calories
30–39 years .... 80 Calories
40–49 years .... 124 Calories
50–59 years .... 1972 Calories
60–69 years .... 7916 Calories
70 and over .... Results are still pending

DRESSING AFTERWARDS:
Calmly .... 32 Calories
In a hurry .... 98 Calories
With her father knocking at the door .... 5218 Calories
With your wife knocking at the door .... 13,521 Calories

Results may vary.

❋ ❋ ❋

Ken's last request…

Ken was on his deathbed and gasped pitifully. "Promise to fulfill my last request, Cindy," he said.

"Of course, Ken," his wife said softly.

"Six months after I die," he said, "I want you to marry Tim."

19

Entertaining!
Amazing!

"But I thought you hated Tim," she said.

With his last breath, Ken said, "I do!"

Larry's bar...

A man goes to a shrink and says, "Doctor, my wife is unfaithful to me. Every evening, she goes to Larry's bar and picks up men. In fact, she goes to bed with anybody who asks her! I'm going crazy. What do you think I should do?"

"Relax," says the Doctor, "take a deep breath and calm down. Now, tell me, where exactly is Larry's bar?"

The curse...

An old man goes to the Wizard to ask him if he can remove a "Curse" he has been living with for the last 40 years.

The Wizard says "Maybe, but you will have to tell me the exact words that were used to put the curse on you."

The old man says without hesitation, "I now pronounce you man and wife."

Man goes to see the Rabbi.

"Rabbi, something terrible is happening and I have to talk to you about it."

The Rabbi asked, "What's wrong?"

The man replied, "My wife is poisoning me."

The Rabbi, very surprised by this, asks, "How can that be?"

The man then pleads, "I'm telling you, I'm certain she's poisoning me. What should I do?"

The Rabbi then offers, "Tell you what. Let me talk to her, I'll see what I can find out and I'll let you know." A week later the Rabbi calls the man and says,

"Well, I spoke to your wife. I spoke to her on the phone for three hours. Do you want to hear my advice?"

The man anxiously says, "YES, YES!"

"Take the poison," says the Rabbi.

✹ ✹ ✹

Dear Tech Support:

Last year I upgraded from Boyfriend 5.0 to Husband 1.0 and noticed a slow-down in the performance of the flower and jewelry applications that had operated flawlessly under the Boyfriend 5.0 system. In addition, Husband 1.0 uninstalled many other "valuable" programs, such as Romance 9.9, and installed "undesir-able" programs such as NFL 7.4, NBA 3.2 and NHL 4.1. Conversation 8.0 also no longer runs, and Housecleaning 2.6 simply crashes the system.

I've tried running Nagging 5.3 to fix these problems, but to no avail.

What can I do?

Signed,

Desperate

Dear Desperate,

First, keep in mind that Boyfriend 5.0 was an entertainment package, while husband 1.0 is an operating system. Try to enter the command C:/ITHOUGHTYOULOVEDME and install Tears 6.2.

Husband 1.0 should then automatically run the applications Guilt 3.3 and Flowers 7.5. But remember, overuse can cause Husband 1.0 to default to such applications as Grumpy Silence 2.5, Happy Hour 7.0, or Beer 6.1.

Please remember that Beer 6.1 is a very bad program that will create SnoringLoudly.WAV files.

Entertaining!
Amazing!

DO NOT install Mother-in-law 1.0 or reinstall another boyfriend program. These are not supported applications, and will crash Husband 1.0. It could also potentially cause Husband 1.0 to default to the program: Girlfriend 9.2, which runs in the background and has been known to introduce potentially serious viruses into the Operating System. In summary, Husband 1.0 is a great program, but it does have limited memory and can't learn new applications quickly. You might consider buying additional software to enhance his system performance. I personally recommend Hot Food 3.0 and Single Malt Scotch 4.5 combined with such applications as that old standby...Lingerie 6.9.

Good Luck,

Tech Support

☀ ☀ ☀

We start to "bud" in our blouses at 9 or 10 years old only to find anything that comes in contact with those tender, blooming buds hurts so bad it brings us to tears. Enter the almighty, uncomfortable training bra contraption the boys in school will snap until we have callouses on our backs.

Next, we get our periods in our early to mid-teens (or sooner). Along with those budding boobs, we now bloat, we cramp, we get the hormone crankies, have to wear little mattresses between our legs or insert tubular, packed cotton rods in places we didn't even know we had.

Our next little rite of passage (premarital or not) is having sex for the first time which is about as much fun as having a ramrod push your uterus through your nostrils (if he did it right and didn't end up with his little cart before his horse), leaving us to wonder what all the fuss was about. Then it's off to Motherhood where we learn to live on dry crackers and water for a few months so we don't

22

Exciting!
Emotional!

spend the entire day leaning over Brother John. Of course, amazing creatures that we are (and we are), we learn to live with the growing little angels inside us steadily kicking our innards night and day making us wonder if we're having Rosemary's Baby. Our once flat bellies now look like we swallowed a watermelon whole and we pee our pants everytime we sneeze.

When the big moment arrives, the dam in our blessed Nether Regions will invariably burst right in the middle of the mall and we'll waddle with our big cartoon feet moaning in pain all the way to the ER. Then it's huff and puff and beg to die while the OB says, "Please stop screaming, Mrs. Hear-me-roar. Calm down and push. Just one more (or 10) good push," warranting a strong, well-deserved impulse to punch the bastard (and hubby) square in the nose for making us cram a wiggling, mushroom-headed 10lb. bowling ball through a keyhole.

After that, it's time to raise those angels only to find that when all that "cute" wears off, the beautiful little darlings morph into walking, jabbering, wet, gooey, snot-blowing, life-sucking little poop machines. The teen years. Need I say more? The kids are almost grown now and we women hit our voracious sexual prime in our mid-30's to early 40's while hubby had his somewhere around his 18th birthday (which just happens to be the reason all that early hot man sex got you pregnant in the first place).

Now we hit the grand finale: "The Menopause," the grandmother of all womanhood. It's either take the HRT and chance cancer in those now seasoned "buds" or the aforementioned Nether Regions, or, sweat like a hog in July, wash your sheets and pillowcases daily and bite the head off anything that moves. Now, you ask WHY women seem to be more spiteful than men when men get off so easy INCLUDING the icing on life's cake: Being able to pee in the woods without soaking their socks...

Entertaining!
Amazing!

Now I love being a woman but "Womanhood" would make the Great Ghandi a tad crabby.

Women are the "weaker sex."

Yeah, right. Bite me.

✸✸✸

Perfect Day for a Woman

8:15 a.m.	Wake up to hugs and kisses.
8:30 a.m.	Weigh 5 lbs. lighter than yesterday.
8:45 a.m.	Breakfast in bed, fresh squeezed orange juice and croissants.
9:15 a.m.	Soothing hot bath with fragrant lilac bath oil.
10:00 a.m.	Light workout at club with handsome, funny personal trainer.
10:30 a.m.	Facial, manicure, shampoo, and comb out.
12:00 noon	Lunch with best friend at an outdoor cafe.
12:45 p.m.	Notice ex-boyfriend's wife, she has gained 30 lbs.
1:00 p.m.	Go out shopping with friends.
3:00 p.m.	Nap.
4:00 p.m.	A dozen roses delivered by florist. Card is from a secret admirer.
4:15 p.m.	Light workout at club followed by a gentle massage.
5:30 p.m.	Pick outfit for dinner. Primp before mirror.
7:30 p.m.	Candlelight dinner for two followed by dancing.
10:00 p.m.	Hot shower. Alone.
10:30 p.m.	Make love.
11:00 p.m.	Pillow talk, light touching and cuddling.
11:15 p.m.	Fall asleep in his big, strong arms.

Exciting!
Emotional!

Perfect Day for a Man

6:00 a.m.	Alarm.
6:15 a.m.	Blowjob.
6:30 a.m.	Massive dump while reading the sports section.
7:00 a.m.	Breakfast. Filet Mignon, eggs, toast and coffee.
7:30 a.m.	Limo arrives.
7:45 a.m.	Bloody Mary en route to airport.
8:15 a.m.	Private jet to Augusta, Georgia.
9:30 a.m.	Limo to Augusta National Golf Club.
9:45 a.m.	Play front nine at Augusta, finish 2 under par.
11:45 a.m.	Lunch. Two dozen oysters on the half shell. Three Heinekens.
12:15 p.m.	Blow job.
12:30 p.m.	Play back nine at Augusta, finish 4 under par.
2:15 p.m.	Limo back to airport. Drink two Bombay martinis.
2:30 p.m.	Private jet to Nassau, Bahamas. Nap.
3:15 p.m.	Late afternoon fishing excursion with topless female crew.
4:30 p.m.	Catch world record light tackle marlin – 1249 lbs.
5:00 p.m.	Jet back home. En route, get massage from naked Kathy Ireland.
7:00 p.m.	Watch CNN Newsflash. Clinton resigns.
7:30 p.m.	Dinner. Lobster appetizers, 1963 Dom Perignon, 20 ounce New York strip steak.
8:00 p.m.	Relax after dinner with 1789 Augler Cognac and Cohiban Cuba cigar.
10:00 p.m.	Have sex with two 18-year-old nymphomaniacs.
11:00 p.m.	Massage and Jacuzzi.
11:45 p.m.	Go to bed.
11:50 p.m.	Let loose a 12 second, four octave fart. Watch the dog leave the room.
11:55 p.m.	Laugh yourself to sleep.

Entertaining!
Amazing!

✻✻✻

The Secret to a Happy Marriage

There was once a man and woman who had been married for more than sixty years. They had shared everything. They had talked about everything. They had kept no secrets from each other except that the little old woman had a shoe box in the top of her closet that she had cautioned her husband never to open or ask her about.

For all of these years, he had never thought about the box, but one day, the little old woman got very sick and the doctor said she would not recover. In trying to sort out their affairs, the little old man took down the shoe box and took it to his wife's bedside. She agreed that it was time that he should know what was in the box.

When he opened it, he found two crocheted doilies and a stack of money totaling $25,000. He asked her about the contents.

"When we were to be married," she said, "my grandmother told me the secret of a happy marriage was to never argue. She told me that if I ever got angry with you I should just keep quiet and crochet a doily."

The little old man was so moved, he had to fight back tears. Only two precious doilies in the box. She had only been angry with him two times in all those years of living and loving. He almost burst with happiness.

"Honey," he said, "that explains the doilies, but what about all of this money? Where did it come from?"

"Oh," she said, "that's the money I made from selling the doilies."

✻✻✻

26

An angel of truth and a dream of fiction,
A woman is a bundle of contradiction,
She's afraid of a wasp, will scream at a mouse,
But will tackle her man alone in the house.
Sour as vinegar, sweet as a rose,
She'll kiss you one minute, then turn up her nose,
She'll win you in rags, enchant you in silk,
She'll be stronger than brandy, milder than milk,
At times she'll be vengeful, merry and sad,
She'll hate you like poison, and love you like mad.

Romance Mathematics

Smart man + smart woman = romance
Smart man + dumb woman = affair
Dumb man + smart woman = marriage
Dumb man + dumb woman = pregnancy

Office Arithmetic

Smart boss + smart employee = profit
Smart boss + dumb employee = production
Dumb boss + smart employee = promotion
Dumb boss + dumb employee = overtime

Entertaining!
Amazing!

Shopping Math

A man will pay $2 for a $1 item he needs.
A woman will pay $1 for a $2 item that she doesn't need.

General Equations & Statistics

A woman worries about the future until she gets a husband.
A man never worries about the future until he gets a wife.
A successful man is one who makes more money than his wife can spend.
A successful woman is one who can find such a man.

Happiness

To be happy with a man, you must understand him a lot and love him a little.
To be happy with a woman, you must love her a lot and not try to understand her at all.

Longevity

Married men live longer than single men, but married men are a lot more willing to die.

Propensity To Change

A woman marries a man expecting he will change, but he doesn't.
A man marries a woman expecting that she won't change, and she does.

Discussion Technique

A woman has the last word in any argument. Anything a man says after that is the beginning of a new argument.

Exciting!
Emotional!

How to Stop People from Bugging You About Getting Married:

Old aunts used to come up to me at weddings, poking me in the ribs and cackling, telling me, "You're next." They stopped after I started doing the same thing to them at funerals.

Send This To A Smart Woman Who Needs A Laugh And To The Guys You Think Can Handle It

☀☀☀

New Drugs For Women!

BUYAGRA: Stimulant to be taken prior to shopping. Increases potency and duration of spending spree.

MENICILLIN: Potent anti-boy-otic for older women. Increases resistance to such lines as, "You make me want to be a better person. Can we get naked now?"

ST. MOM'S WORT: Plant extract that treats mom's depression by rendering preschoolers unconscious for up to six hours.

EMPTY NESTROGEN: Highly effective supplement that eliminates melancholy by enhancing the memory of how awful they were as teenagers and how you couldn't wait till they moved out.

PEPTO-BIMBO: Liquid silicone for single women. Two full cups swallowed before an evening out increases breast size, decreases intelligence, and improves flirting.

DUMMEROL: When taken with Pepto-bimbo, can cause lowering of IQ, causing enjoyment of loud country music and cheap beer.

Entertaining!
Amazing!

FLIPITOR: Increases life expectancy of commuters by controlling road rage and the urge to flip off other drivers.

JACKASSPIRIN: Relieves headache caused by a man who can't remember your birthday, anniversary, or phone number.

ANTI-TALKSIDENT: A spray carried in a purse or wallet to be used on anyone too eager to share their life stories with total strangers.

RAGAMET: When administered to a husband, provides the same irritation as nagging on him all weekend, saving the wife the time and trouble of doing it herself.

DAMMITOL: Take two and the rest of the world can go to hell for 8 hours!

✴ ✴ ✴

Wife quotes

Every man should get married some time; after all, happiness is not the only thing in life!!
—Anonymous

An archaeologist is the best husband a woman can have; the older she gets the more interested he is in her.
—Agatha Christie

Bachelors should be heavily taxed. It is not fair that some men should be happier than others.
—Oscar Wilde

Exciting!
Emotional!

Don't marry for money, you can borrow it cheaper.
—Scottish Proverb

I don't worry about terrorism. I was married for two years.
—Sam Kinison

A psychiatrist is a person who will give you expensive answers that your wife will give you for free.
—Anonymous

Bachelors know more about women than married men. If they didn't, they'd be married too.
—H.L. Mencken

Men have a better time than women. For one thing, they marry later, for another thing, they die earlier.
—H.L. Mencken

"A man without a woman is like a fish without a bicycle."
—U2

Marriage is a three ring circus:
—engagement ring
—wedding ring
—suffering

When a newly married couple smiles, everyone knows why.
When a ten-year married couple smiles, everyone wonders why.

Love is blind but marriage is an eye-opener.

31

When a man opens the door of his car for his wife, you can be sure of one thing: either the car is new or the wife.

If your dog is barking at the back door and your wife is yelling at the front door, who do you let in first?

The dog of course…at least he'll shut up after you let him in!

A man placed some flowers on the grave of his dearly departed mother and started back toward his car when his attention was diverted to another man kneeling at a grave. The man seemed to be praying with profound intensity and kept repeating, "Why did you have to die? Why did you have to die?" The first man approached him and said,

"Sir, I don't wish to interfere with your private grief, but this demonstration of pain is more than I've ever seen before. For whom do you mourn so deeply? A child? A parent?"

The mourner took a moment to collect himself, then replied,

"My wife's first husband."

A couple came upon a wishing well. The husband leaned over, made a wish and threw in a penny. The wife decided to make a wish, too. But she leaned over too much, fell into the well and drowned.

The husband was stunned for a while but then smiled.

"It really works!"

Exciting!
Emotional!

Chapter 2

Animal, Blonde, Church Humor

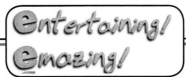

World's Funniest and Greatest E-mails

DOG'S DIARY

DAY 180
8:00 a.m. – OH BOY! DOG FOOD! MY FAVORITE!
9:30 a.m. – OH BOY! A CAR RIDE! MY FAVORITE!
9:40 a.m. – OH BOY! A WALK! MY FAVORITE!
10:30 a.m. – OH BOY! A CAR RIDE! MY FAVORITE!
11:30 a.m. – OH BOY! DOG FOOD! MY FAVORITE!
12:00 noon – OH BOY! THE KIDS! MY FAVORITE!
1:00 p.m. – OH BOY! THE YARD! MY FAVORITE!
4:00 p.m. – OH BOY! THE KIDS! MY FAVORITE!
5:00 p.m. – OH BOY! DOG FOOD! MY FAVORITE!
5:30 p.m. – OH BOY! MOM! MY FAVORITE!

DAY 181
8:00 a.m. – OH BOY! DOG FOOD! MY FAVORITE!
9:30 a.m. – OH BOY! A CAR RIDE! MY FAVORITE!
9:40 a.m. – OH BOY! A WALK! MY FAVORITE!
10:30 a.m. – OH BOY! A CAR RIDE! MY FAVORITE!
11:30 a.m. – OH BOY! DOG FOOD! MY FAVORITE!
12:00 noon – OH BOY! THE KIDS! MY FAVORITE!
1:00 p.m. – OH BOY! THE YARD! MY FAVORITE!
4:00 p.m. – OH BOY! THE KIDS! MY FAVORITE!
5:00 p.m. – OH BOY! DOG FOOD! MY FAVORITE!
5:30 p.m. – OH BOY! MOM! MY FAVORITE!

Exciting!
Emotional!

DAY 182
8:00 a.m. – OH BOY! DOG FOOD! MY FAVORITE!
9:30 a.m. – OH BOY! A CAR RIDE! MY FAVORITE!
9:40 a.m. – OH BOY! A WALK! MY FAVORITE!
10:30 a.m. – OH BOY! A CAR RIDE! MY FAVORITE!
11:30 a.m. – OH BOY! DOG FOOD! MY FAVORITE!
12:00 noon – OH BOY! THE KIDS! MY FAVORITE!
1:00 p.m. – OH BOY! THE YARD! MY FAVORITE!
1:30 p.m. – ooooooo. bath. bummer.
4:00 p.m. – OH BOY! THE KIDS! MY FAVORITE!
5:00 p.m. – OH BOY! DOG FOOD! MY FAVORITE!
5:30 p.m. – OH BOY! MOM! MY FAVORITE!

Excerpts from a Cat's Diary

DAY 752

My captors continue to taunt me with bizarre little dangling objects. They dine lavishly on fresh meat, while I am forced to eat dry cereal. The only thing that keeps me going is the hope of escape, and the mild satisfaction I get from ruining the occasional piece of furniture. Tomorrow I may eat another houseplant.

DAY 761

Today my attempt to kill my captors by weaving around their feet while they were walking almost succeeded, tried this at the top of the stairs. In an attempt to disgust and repulse these vile oppressors, I once again induced myself to vomit on their favorite chair…must try this on their bed.

35

Entertaining!
Amazing!

DAY 765

Decapitated a mouse and brought them the headless body, in attempt to make them aware of what I am capable of and to try to strike fear into their hearts. They only "cooed" and condescended about what a good little cat I was... Hmmm. Not working according to plan.

DAY 768

I am finally aware of how sadistic they are. For no good reason I was chosen for the water torture. This time however it included a burning, foamy chemical called "shampoo." What sick minds could invent such a liquid? My only consolation is the piece of thumb still stuck between my teeth.

DAY 771

There was some sort of gathering of their accomplices. I was placed in solitary throughout the event. However, I could hear the noise and smell the foul odor of the glass tubes they call "beer..." More importantly, I overheard that my confinement was due to MY power of "allergies." Must learn what this is and how to use it.

DAY 774

I am convinced the other captives are flunkies and maybe snitches. The dog is routinely released and seems more than happy to return. He is obviously a half-wit. The bird on the other hand has got to be an informant, and speaks with them regularly. I am certain he reports my every move. Due to his current placement in the metal room his safety is assured. But I can wait, it is only a matter of time...

❋❋❋

Exciting!
Emotional!

Once upon a time, allegedly, in a nice little forest, there lived an orphaned bunny and an orphaned snake. By a surprising coincidence, both were blind from birth.

One day, the bunny was hopping through the forest, and the snake was slithering through the forest, when the bunny tripped over the snake and fell down. This, of course, knocked the snake about quite a bit.

"Oh, my," said the bunny, "I'm terribly sorry. I didn't mean to hurt you. I've been blind since birth, so, I can't see where I'm going. In fact, since I'm also an orphan, I don't even know what I am."

"It's quite OK," replied the snake. "Actually, my story is much the same as yours. I, too, have been blind since birth and also never knew my mother. Tell you what, maybe I could slither all over you, and work out what you are, so at least you'll have that going for you…"

"Oh, that would be wonderful" replied the bunny.

So the snake slithered all over the bunny, and said, "Well, you're covered with soft fur; you have really long ears; your nose twitches; and you have a soft cottony tail. I'd say that you must be a bunny rabbit."

"Oh, thank you! Thank you," cried the bunny, in obvious excitement.

The bunny suggested to the snake, "Maybe I could feel you all over with my paw, and help you the same way that you've helped me."

So the bunny felt the snake all over, and remarked, "Well, you're smooth and slippery, and you have a forked tongue, no backbone and no balls. I'd say you must be either a politician, a team leader or possibly someone in senior management."

❋ ❋ ❋

Entertaining!
Amazing!

World's Funniest and Greatest E-mails

A man walks into the pet store and goes up to the service assistant. "Excuse me, I want a pet, but not just any pet, a really unusual pet."

The service assistant says "I have just the thing for you, it's a talking centipede."

"Cool!" the man exclaims, "I'll take it!"

The man takes the centipede home in its little box and places him on the kitchen table. He looks into the box and says, "Hey centipede, what about you and me going to the pub for a beer?"

The centipede doesn't answer, so the guy thinks, "I'll just go off for five minutes and come back and ask again."

Five minutes pass and the guy returns to the centipede. "Hey centipede, how about you and me go to the pub for a beer?"

Again, the centipede doesn't answer him. "Hmmmmm" the guy thinks to himself, "I'll just go off and watch this TV show, come back and ask him again."

Half an hour passes and the guy returns to the centipede. "I'll just ask him one more time" he tells himself. "Hey centipede, how about you and me go to the pub for a beer?"

The centipede looks up at the man and says, "Damn it, I heard you the first time, I'm putting my shoes on!"

✺✺✺

A chicken and an egg are lying in bed. The chicken is leaning against the headboard, a satisfied smile on its face. The egg, looking a bit irritated, grabs the sheet, rolls over, and says:

"Well, I guess we finally answered THAT question!"

✷✷✷

Just after dinner one night, my son came up to tell me there was "something wrong" with one of the two hamsters he holds prisoner in his room. "He's just lying there looking sick," he told me. "I'm serious, Dad. Can you help?"

I put my best hamster-healer statement on my face and followed him into his bedroom. One of the little rodents was indeed lying on his back, looking stressed. I immediately knew what to do. "Honey," I called, "come look at the hamster!"

"Oh, my gosh," my wife diagnosed after a minute. "She's having babies."

"What?" my son demanded. "But their names are Bert and Ernie, Mom!"

I was equally outraged. "Hey, how can that be? I thought we said we didn't want them to reproduce," I accused my wife.

"Well, what do you want me to do, post a sign in their cage,?" she inquired. (I actually think she said this sarcastically!)

"No, but you were supposed to get two boys!" I reminded her, (in my most loving, calm, sweet voice, while gritting my teeth together).

"Yeah, Bert and Ernie!" my son agreed.

"Well, it's just a little hard to tell on some guys, you know," she informed me. Again with the sarcasm, ya think?)

By now the rest of the family had gathered to see what was going on. I shrugged, deciding to make the best of it. "Kids, this is going to be a wondrous experience, I announced. "We're about to witness the miracle of birth."

"OH, gross!", they shrieked.

"Well, isn't THAT just Great! What are we going to do with a litter of tiny little hamster babies?" my wife wanted to know. (I really do think she was being snotty here, too, don't you?)

39

Entertaining!
Amazing!

We peered at the patient. After much struggling, what looked like a tiny foot would appear briefly, vanishing a scant second later.

"We don't appear to be making much progress," I noted.

"It's breech," my wife whispered, horrified. "Do something, Dad!" my son urged.

"Okay, okay." Squeamishly, I reached in and grabbed the foot when it next appeared, giving it a gingerly tug. It disappeared. I tried several more times with the same results.

"Should I call 911?" my eldest daughter wanted to know. "Maybe they could talk us through the trauma." (You see a pattern here with the females in my house?)

"Let's get Ernie to the vet," I said grimly. We drove to the vet with my son holding the cage in his lap.

"Breathe, Ernie, breathe," he urged.

"I don't think hamsters do Lamaze," his mother noted to him. (Women can be so cruel to their own young. I mean what she does to me is one thing, but this boy is of her womb, for God's sake.)

The vet took Ernie back to the examining room and peered at the little animal through a magnifying glass. "What do you think, Doc, a c-section?" I suggested scientifically. "Oh, very interesting," he murmured.

"Mr. and Mrs. Cameron, may I speak to you privately for a moment?" I gulped, nodding for my son to step outside.

"Is Ernie going to be okay?" my wife asked.

"Oh, perfectly," the vet assured us. "This hamster is not in labor. In fact, that isn't EVER going to happen…Ernie is a boy."

"What?"

40

Exciting!
Emotional!

"You see, Ernie is a young male. And occasionally, as they come into maturity, like most male species, they um…er…masturbate. Just the way he did, lying on his back." He blushed, glancing at my wife.

"Well, you know what I'm saying, Mr…Cameron."

We were silent, absorbing this. "So Ernie's just…just…excited?" my wife offered.

"Exactly," the vet replied, relieved that we understood. More silence. Then my viscous, cruel wife started to giggle. And giggle. And then even laugh loudly.

"What's so funny?" I demanded, knowing, but not believing that the woman I married would commit the upcoming affront to my flawless manliness. Tears were now running down her face.

"It's just…that…I'm picturing you pulling on its…its…teeny little…" she gasped for more air to bellow in laughter once more.

"That's enough," I warned.

We thanked the Veterinarian and hurriedly bundled the hamsters and our son back into the car. He was glad everything was going to be okay. "I know Ernie's really thankful for what you've done, Dad," he told me.

"Oh, you have NO idea," my wife agreed, collapsing with laughter.

2 – Hamsters	$10…
1 – Cage	$20…
Trip to the Vet	$30…

Pictures of your hubby pulling on the hamster's wacker…Priceless!

☀☀☀

Entertaining!
Amazing!

A New Zealander buys several sheep, hoping to breed them for wool. After several weeks, he notices that none of the sheep are getting pregnant, and calls a vet for help. The vet tells him that he should try artificial insemination. The farmer doesn't have the slightest idea what this means but, not wanting to display his ignorance, only asks the vet how he will know when the sheep are pregnant. The vet tells him that they will stop standing around and instead will lie down and wallow in grass when they are pregnant.

The man hangs up and gives it some thought. He comes to the conclusion that artificial insemination means he has to impregnate the sheep. So, he loads the sheep into his Landrover, drives them out into the woods, has sex with them all, brings them back and goes to bed.

Next morning, he wakes and looks out at the sheep. Seeing that they are all still standing around, he deduces that the first try didn't take, and loads them in the Landrover again. He drives them out to the woods, bangs each sheep twice for good measure brings them back and goes to bed exhausted.

Next morning, he wakes to find the sheep still just standing round. One more try, he tells himself, and proceeds to load them up and drive them out to the woods. He spends all day shagging the sheep and, upon returning home, falls listlessly into bed.

The next morning, he cannot even raise himself from the bed to look at the sheep. He asks his wife to look out and tell him if the sheep are lying in the grass. "No," she says, "they're all in the Landrover and one of them is beeping the horn.

☀ ☀ ☀

A couple made a deal that whoever died first would come back and inform the other of the afterlife. Their biggest fear was that there was no heaven.

42

exciting!
emotional!

After a long life, the husband was the first to go, and true to his word, he made contact.

"Mary...Mary..."

"Is that you, Fred?"

"Yes, I've come back like we agreed."

"What's it like?"

"Well, I get up in the morning, I have sex. I have breakfast, I have sex. I bathe in the sun, then I have sex twice. I have lunch, then sex pretty much all afternoon. After supper, I have sex until late at night. The next day it starts again."

"Oh, Fred you surely must be in heaven."

"Not exactly, I'm a rabbit in Oklahoma.

※※※

If you're a bear, you get to hibernate. You do nothing but sleep for six months. I could deal with that.

Before you hibernate, you're supposed to eat like crazy. I could deal with that, too.

If you're a bear, you birth your children (who are the size of walnuts) while you're sleeping and wake to partially grown, cute, cuddly cubs. I could definitely deal with that.

If you're a mama bear, everyone knows you mean business. You swat anyone who bothers your cubs. If your cubs get out of line, you swat them too. I could deal with that.

If you're a bear, your mate EXPECTS you to wake up growling. He EXPECTS that you will have hairy legs and excess body fat.

Yep...I wanna be a bear.

43

※ ※ ※

In light of our world situation, this is profound.

This is a very simplistic story, but a powerful message.

A mouse looked through a crack in the wall to see the farmer and his wife opening a package. What food might it contain?

He was aghast to discover that it was a mouse trap!

Retreating to the farmyard, the mouse proclaimed the warning, "There is a mouse trap in the house, there is a mouse trap in the house."

The chicken clucked and scratched, raised her head and said, "Mr. Mouse, I can tell you this is a grave concern to you, but it is of no consequence to me. I cannot be bothered by it."

The mouse turned to the pig and told him, "There is a mouse trap in the house!"

"I am so very sorry Mr. Mouse," sympathized the pig, "but there is nothing I can do about it but pray; be assured that you are in my prayers."

The mouse turned to the cow, who replied, "Like wow, Mr. Mouse, a mouse trap. Am I in grave danger? Duh."

So the mouse returned to the house, head down and dejected to face the farmer's mouse trap alone.

That very night a sound was heard throughout the house, like the sound of a mouse trap catching its prey. The farmer's wife rushed to see what was caught.

In the darkness, she did not see that it was a venomous snake whose tail the trap had caught.

The snake bit the farmer's wife.

The farmer rushed her to the hospital.

Exciting! Emotional!

She returned home with a fever.

Now everyone knows you treat a fever with fresh chicken soup, so the farmer took his hatchet to the farmyard for the soup's main ingredient.

His wife's sickness continued so that friends and neighbors came to sit with her around the clock. To feed them, the farmer butchered the pig.

The farmer's wife did not get well, in fact, she died, and so many people came for her funeral the farmer had the cow slaughtered to provide meat for all of them to eat.

So the next time you hear that someone is facing a problem and think that it does not concern you, remember that when the least of us is threatened, we are all at risk.

❋❋❋

1. The later you are, the more excited they are to see you.
2. Dogs will forgive you for playing with other dogs.
3. If a dog is gorgeous, other dogs don't hate it.
4. Dogs don't notice if you call them by another dog's name.
5. A dog's disposition stays the same all month long.
6. Dogs like it if you leave a lot of things on the floor.
7. A dog's parents never visit.
8. Dogs do not hate their bodies.
9. Dogs agree that you have to raise your voice to get your point across.
10. Dogs like to do their snooping outside rather than in your wallet or desk.
11. Dogs seldom outlive you.
12. Dogs can't talk.
13. Dogs enjoy petting in public.

Entertaining!
Amazing!

14. You never have to wait for a dog; they're ready to go 24-hours a day.
15. Dogs find you amusing when you're drunk.
16. Dogs like to go hunting.
17. Another man will seldom steal your dog.
18. If you bring another dog home, your dog will happily play with both of you.
19. A dog will not wake you up at night to ask, "If I died would you get another dog?"
20. If you pretend to be blind, your dog can stay in your hotel room for free.
21. If a dog has babies, you can put an ad in the paper and give them away.
22. A dog will let you put a studded collar on it without calling you a pervert.
23. A dog won't hold out on you to get a new car.
24. If a dog smells another dog on you, they don't get mad, they just think it's interesting.
25. If you are going out, your dog is always ready.
26. Dogs don't let magazine articles guide their lives.
27. When your dog gets old, you can have it put to sleep.
28. Dogs like to ride in the back of a pickup truck.
29. Dogs are not allowed in Bloomingdale's or Neiman-Marcus.
30. If a dog leaves, it won't take half your stuff.

❋❋❋

"Inner Strength"

If you can start the day without caffeine or pep pills,
If you can be cheerful, ignoring aches and pains,
If you can resist complaining and boring people with your troubles,
If you can eat the same food everyday and be grateful for it,

Exciting!
Emotional!

If you can understand when loved ones are too busy to give you time,
If you can overlook when people take things out on you when, through no
fault of yours, something goes wrong,
If you can take criticism and blame without resentment,
If you can face the world without lies and deceit,
If you can conquer tension without medical help,
If you can relax without liquor,
If you can sleep without the aid of drugs,
If you can do all these things,

Then you are probably the family dog.

☀☀☀

For all of you dog lovers out there, some of life's truths.

"The reason a dog has so many friends is that he wags his tail instead of his tongue." —Anonymous

"Don't accept your dog's admiration as conclusive evidence that you are wonderful." —Ann Landers

"If there are no dogs in Heaven, then when I die I want to go where they went." —Will Rogers

"There is no psychiatrist in the world like a puppy licking your face." —Ben Williams

"A dog is the only thing on earth that loves you more than he loves himself". —Josh Billings

Entertaining!
Amazing!

"The average dog is a nicer person than the average person." —Andrew A. Rooney

"We give dogs time we can spare, space we can spare and love we can spare. And in return, dogs give us their all. It's the best deal man has ever made." —M. Acklam

"Dogs love their friends and bite their enemies, quite unlike people, who are incapable of pure love and always have to mix love and hate." —Sigmund Freud

"I wonder what goes through his mind when he sees us peeing in his water bowl." —Penny Ward Moser

"A dog teaches a boy fidelity, perseverance and to turn around three times before lying down." —Robert Benchley

"Dogs need to sniff the ground; it's how they keep abreast of current events. The ground is a giant dog newspaper, containing all kinds of late-breaking dog news items, which, if they are especially urgent, are often continued in the next yard." —Dave Barry

"Anybody who doesn't know what soap tastes like never washed a dog." —Franklin P. Jones

"If I have any beliefs about immortality, it is that certain dogs I have known will go to heaven, and very, very few persons." —James Thurber

"If your dog is fat, you aren't getting enough exercise." —Unknown

*Exciting!
Emotional!*

"Ever consider what they must think of us? I mean, here we come back from a grocery store with the most amazing haul—chicken, pork, half a cow. They must think we're the greatest hunters on earth!" —Anne Tyler

✹✹✹

Notice to people who visit my home:

1. The dogs live here. You don't.

2. If you don't want dog hair on your clothes, stay off the furniture.

3. Yes, they have some disgusting habits. So do I and so do you. What's your point?

4. OF COURSE they smell like a dog.

5. It's their nature to try to sniff your crotch. Please feel free to sniff theirs.

6. I like them a lot better than I like most people.

7. To you they're a dog. To me they're adopted children, who are short, hairy, walk on all fours and don't speak clearly. I have no problem with any of these things.

8. Dogs are better than kids. They eat less, don't ask for money all the time, are easier to train, usually come when called, never drive your car, don't hang out with drug-using friends, don't smoke or drink, don't worry about whether they have the latest fashions, don't wear your clothes, don't need a gazillion dollars for college, and if they get pregnant, you can sell the pups.

9. The same applies for the cats, except they will ignore you…until you're asleep.

✹✹✹

49

Entertaining! Amazing!

The Ant and the Grasshopper

Classic Version:

The ant works hard in the withering heat all summer long, building his house and laying up supplies for the winter. The grasshopper thinks he's a fool and laughs and dances and plays the summer away. Come winter, the ant is warm and well fed.

The grasshopper has no food or shelter so he dies out in the cold.

Moral of the Story: Be responsible for yourself!

Modern Version:

The ant works hard in the withering heat all summer long, building his house and laying up supplies for the winter. The grasshopper thinks he's a fool and laughs and dances and plays the summer away.

Come winter, the shivering grasshopper calls a press conference and demands to know why the ant should be allowed to be warm and well fed while others are cold and starving.

CBS, NBC, ABC, and CNN show up to provide pictures of the shivering grasshopper next to a video of the ant in his comfortable home with a table filled with food.

America is stunned by the sharp contrast. How can this be, that in a country of such wealth, this poor grasshopper is allowed to suffer so?

Kermit the Frog appears on Oprah with the grasshopper, and everybody cries when they sing "It's Not Easy Being Green."

Jesse Jackson stages a demonstration in front of the ant's house where the news stations film the group singing "We shall overcome". Jesse then has the group kneel down to pray to God for the grasshopper's sake.

Exciting!
Emotional!

Tom Daschle and Walter Mondale exclaim in an interview with Peter Jennings that the ant has gotten rich off the back of the grasshopper, and both call for an immediate tax hike on the ant to make him pay his "fair share".

Finally, the EEOC drafts the "Economic Equity and Anti-Grasshopper Act", retroactive to the beginning of the summer. The ant is fined for failing to hire a proportionate number of green bugs and, having nothing left to pay his retroactive taxes, his home is confiscated by the government.

Hillary gets her old law firm to represent the grasshopper in a defamation suit against the ant, and the case is tried before a panel of federal judges that Bill appointed from a list of single-parent welfare recipients.

The ant loses the case.

The story ends as we see the grasshopper finishing up the last bits of the ant's food while the government house he is in, which just happens to be the ant's old house, crumbles around him because he doesn't maintain it.

The ant has disappeared in the snow.

The grasshopper is found dead in a drug-related incident and the house, now abandoned, is taken over by a gang of spiders who terrorize the once peaceful neighborhood.

Moral of the Story: Vote Republican

☀☀☀

The Origin of PETS

A newly discovered chapter in the Book of Genesis has provided the answer to "Where do pets come from?"

51

Entertaining!
Amazing!

Adam and Eve said, "Lord, when we were in the garden, you walked with us every day. Now we do not see you any more. We are lonesome here, and it is difficult for us to remember how much you love us."

And God said, "No problem! I will create a companion for you that will be with you forever and who will be a reflection of my love for you, so that you will love me even when you cannot see me. Regardless of how selfish or childish or unlovable you may be, this new companion will accept you as you are and will love you as I do, in spite of yourselves."

And God created a new animal to be a companion for Adam and Eve.

And it was a good animal.

And God was pleased.

And the new animal was pleased to be with Adam and Eve and he wagged his tail.

And Adam said, "Lord, I have already named all the animals in the Kingdom and I cannot think of a name for this new animal."

And God said, "No problem. Because I have created this new animal to be a reflection of my love for you, his name will be a reflection of my own name, and you will call him DOG."

And Dog lived with Adam and Eve and was a companion to them and loved them.

And they were comforted.

And God was pleased.

And Dog was content and wagged his tail.

After a while, it came to pass that an angel came to the Lord and said, "Lord, Adam and Eve have become filled with pride. They strut and preen like peacocks and they believe they are worthy of adoration. Dog has indeed taught them that they are loved, but perhaps too well."

52

Exciting!
Emotional!

And God said, "No problem! I will create for them a companion who will be with them forever and who will see them as they are. The companion will remind them of their limitations, so they will know that they are not always worthy of adoration."

And God created CAT to be a companion to Adam and Eve.

And Cat would not obey them. And when Adam and Eve gazed into Cat's eyes, they were reminded that they were not the supreme beings.

And Adam and Eve learned humility.

And they were greatly improved.

And God was pleased.

And Dog was happy.

And Cat didn't give a shit one way or the other.

☀☀☀

Dog Pet Peeves

- Blaming your farts on me…not funny.
- Yelling at me for barking…I am a dog you moron, what am I supposed to do?
- How you naively believe that the stupid cat isn't all over everything while you're gone. (Have you noticed that your toothbrush tastes a little like cat?)
- Taking me for a walk, then not letting me check stuff out. Exactly whose damn walk is this anyway?
- Any trick that involves balancing food on my nose…stop it.
- Yelling at me for rubbing my ass on your carpet. Why'd you buy carpet?

53

Entertaining!
Amazing!

- Getting upset when I sniff the crotches of your guests. Sorry but I haven't quite mastered that handshake thing yet.
- How you act disgusted when I lick myself. Look, we both know the truth, you're just jealous.
- Dog sweaters. Have you noticed my fur?
- Any haircut that involves bows or ribbons. Now you know why we chew your stuff up when you're not home.
- Taking me to the vet for "the big snip," then acting surprised when I freak out every time we go back there.
- The sleight of hand, fake fetch throw. You fooled a dog! What a proud moment for the top of the food chain.

☀☀☀

A blind man enters a Women's Bar by mistake. He finds his way to a bar stool and orders a drink. After sitting there for a while, he yells to the bartender, "Hey, you wanna hear a blonde joke?"

The bar immediately falls absolutely quiet. In a very deep, husky voice, the woman next to him says, "Before you tell that joke, sir, you should know five things:

1 – The bartender is a blonde girl.
2 – The bouncer is a blonde gal.
3 – I'm a 6 foot tall, 200 pound blonde woman with a black belt in karate.
4 – The woman sitting next to me is blonde and is a professional weightlifter.
5 – The lady to your right is a blonde and is a professional wrestler.

Now think about it seriously, Mister. Do you still wanna tell that joke?

The blind man thinks for a second, shakes his head, and declares, "Nah…Not if I'm gonna have to explain it five times."

☀☀☀

A blond girl comes back from school one evening. She runs to her mum and says: "Mummy today at school we learnt how to count. Well, all the other girls only counted to 5, but listen to me: 1, 2, 3, 4, 5, 6, 7, 8, 9, 10 ! It's good, innit?"

"Yes, darling, very good."

"Is that because I'm blond?"

"Yes, darling, it's because you're blond."

Next day, the little girl comes back from school and says: "Mummy, today at school we learnt the alphabet. All the other girls only went as far as D, but listen to me: A, B, C, D, E, F, G, H, I, J, K ! It's good, innit?"

"Yes, darling, very good."

"Is that because I'm blond, mummy?"

"Yes, darling it's because you're blond."

Next Day, she returns from school and cries: "Mummy, today we went swimming. Well, all the other girls have no breasts, but look at me!" She proceeds to flash her breasts at her mummy. "Is that because I'm blond, mummy?"

"No darling, it's because you're 25."

☀☀☀

A blonde, wanting to earn some extra money, decided to hire herself out as a "handy-woman" and started canvassing a nearby well-to-do neighborhood.

She went to the front door of the first house, and asked the owner if he had any odd jobs for her to do. "Well, I guess I could use somebody to paint my porch," he said. "How much will you charge me?" The blonde quickly responded, "How about $50?"

The man agreed and told her that the paint and everything she would need were in the garage.

The man's wife, hearing the conversation, said to her husband, "Does she realize that our porch goes all the way around the house?" He responded, "That's a bit cynical, isn't it?"

The wife replied, "You're right. I guess I'm starting to believe all those 'dumb blonde' jokes we've been getting by e-mail lately."

A short time later, the blonde came to the door to collect her money.

"You're finished already?" the husband asked.

Yes," the blonde replied, "and I had paint left over, so I gave it two coats."

Impressed, the man reached into his pocket for the $50.00 and handed it to her.

And by the way," the blonde added, "it's not a Porch, it's a Lexus"

❋❋❋

A blonde girl enters a store that sells curtains.
She tells the salesman:
"I would like to buy a pink curtain in the size of my computer screen."
The surprised salesman replies:
"But, madam, computers do not have curtains!!!"
…And the blonde said:
"Helloooo…? I've got Windows"!!!

❋❋❋

Exciting!
Emotional!

❁ ❁ ❁

Seven degrees of blondness

First Degree: A married couple were asleep when the phone rang at 2 in the morning. The wife (undoubtedly blonde), picked up the phone, listened a moment and said, "How should I know, that's 200 miles from here!" and hung up. The husband said, "Who was that?" The wife said, "I don't know, some woman wanting to know if the coast is clear."

Second Degree: Two blondes are walking down the street. One notices a compact on the sidewalk and leans down to pick it up. She opens it, looks in the mirror and says, "Hmm, this person looks familiar." The second blonde says, "Here, let me see!" So the first blonde hands her the compact. The second one looks in the mirror and says, "You dummy, it's me!"

Third Degree: A blonde suspects her boyfriend of cheating on her, so she goes out and buys a gun. She goes to his apartment unexpectedly and when she opens the door she finds him in the arms of a redhead. Well, the blonde is really angry. She opens her purse to take out the gun, and as she does so, she is overcome with grief. She takes the gun and puts it to her head. The boyfriend yells, "No, honey, don't do it!!!" The blonde replies, "Shut up, you're next!"

Fourth Degree: A blonde was bragging about her knowledge of state capitals. She proudly says, "Go ahead, ask me, I know all of them." A friend says, "OK, what's the capital of Wisconsin?" The blonde replies, "Oh, that's easy: W."

Fifth Degree: What did the blonde ask her doctor when he told her she was pregnant? "Is it mine?"

Entertaining!
Amazing!

Sixth Degree: Bambi, a blonde in her fourth year as a UCLA freshman, sat in her US government class. The professor asked Bambi if she knew what Roe vs. Wade was about. Bambi pondered the question then finally said, "That was the decision George Washington had to make before he crossed the Delaware."

Seventh Degree: Returning home from work, a blonde was shocked to find her house ransacked and burglarized. She telephoned the police at once and reported the crime. The police dispatcher broadcast the call on the radio, and a K-9 unit, patrolling nearby was the first to respond. As the K-9 officer approached the house with his dog on a leash, the blonde ran out on the porch, shuddered at the sight of the cop and his dog, then sat down on the steps. Putting her face in her hands, she moaned, "I come home to find all my possessions stolen. I call the police for help, and what do they do? They send me a BLIND policeman."

Auto Repair

A blonde pushes her BMW into a gas station. She tells the mechanic it died. After he works on it for a few minutes, it is idling smoothly.

She says, "What's the story?"

He replies, "Just crap in the carburetor."

She asks, "How often do I have to do that?"

Speeding Ticket

A police officer stops a blonde for speeding and asks her very nicely if he could see her license.

She replied in a huff, "I wish you guys would get your act together. Just yesterday you take away my license and then today you expect me to show it to you!"

Exciting!
Emotional!

Exposure

A blonde is walking down the street with her blouse open and her right breast hanging out. A policeman approaches her and says, "Ma'am, are you aware that I could cite you for indecent exposure?"

She says, "Why, officer?"

"Because your breast is hanging out." he says.

She looks down and says, "OH, MY GOD! I left the baby on the bus again!"

River Walk

There's this blonde out for a walk. She comes to a river and sees another blonde on the opposite bank.

"Yoo-hoo!" she shouts, "How can I get to the other side?"

The second blonde looks up the river then down the river and shouts back, "You ARE on the other side."

Knitting

A highway patrolman pulled alongside a speeding car on the freeway.

Glancing at the car, he was astounded to see that the blonde behind the wheel was knitting! Realizing that she was oblivious to his flashing lights and siren, the trooper cranked down his window, turned on his bullhorn and yelled, "PULL OVER!"

"NO!" the blonde yelled back, "IT'S A SCARF!"

Blonde on the Sun

A Russian, an American, and a Blonde were talking one day.

The Russian said, 'We were the first in space!'

The American said, "We were the first on the moon!"

The Blonde said, "So what? We're going to be the first on the sun!"

Entertaining!
Amazing!

The Russian and the American looked at each other and shook their heads.

"You can't land on the sun, you idiot! You'll burn up!" said the Russian.

To which the Blonde replied, "We're not stupid, you know. We're going at night!"

In A Vacuum

A blonde was playing Trivial Pursuit one night. It was her turn.

She rolled the dice and she landed on Science & Nature. Her question was, "If you are in a vacuum and someone calls your name, can you hear it?"

She thought for a time and then asked, "Is it on or off?"

Final Exam

The blonde reported for her university final examination that consists of yes/no type questions. She takes her seat in the examination hall, stares at the question paper for five minutes and then, in a fit of inspiration, takes out her purse, removes a coin and starts tossing the coin, marking the answer sheet:

Yes, for Heads, and No, for Tails.

Within half an hour she is all done, whereas the rest of the class is still sweating it out. During the last few minutes she is seen desperately throwing the coin, muttering and sweating. The moderator, alarmed, approaches her and asks what is going on. "I finished the exam in half an hour, but now I'm rechecking my answers."

Exciting!
Emotional!

Finally, the blonde joke to end all blonde jokes!

There was a blonde woman who was having financial troubles so she decided to kidnap a child and demand a ransom. She went to a local park, grabbed a little boy, took him behind a tree and wrote this note:

I have kidnapped your child. Leave $10,000 in a plain brown bag behind the big oak tree in the park tomorrow at 7 A.M.

Signed,

The Blonde

She pinned the note inside the little boy's jacket and told him to go straight home. The next morning, she returned to the park to find the $10,000 in a brown bag behind the big oak tree, just as she had instructed. Inside the bag was the following note...

Here is your money. I cannot believe that one blonde would do this to another!

❄ ❄ ❄

She thought a quarterback was a refund.
She thought General Motors was in the Army.
She thought Meow Mix was a CD for cats.
She thought Boyz II Men was a day-care centre.
At the bottom of an application where it says "sign here," she wrote "Sagittarius."
She took a ruler to bed to see how long she slept.
She sent a fax with a stamp on it.
She thought Eartha Kitt was a set of garden tools.
She thought TuPac Shakur was a Jewish holiday.
Under "education" on her job application, she put "Hooked on Phonics".

Entertaining!
Amazing!

She tripped over a cordless phone.

She spent 20 minutes looking at an orange juice can because it said "Concentrate."

She told someone to meet her at the corner of "WALK" and "DON'T WALK."

She asked for a price check at the Dollar Store.

She tried to put M&M's in alphabetical order.

She studied for a blood test.

She thought she needed a token to get on "Soul Train."

She sold the car for gas money.

When she missed the 44 bus, she took the 22 bus twice instead.

When she went to the airport and saw a sign that said, "Airport Left," she turned around and went home.

When she heard that 90% of all crimes occur around the home, she moved.

She thought Taco Bell was Mexico's phone company.

She thought if she spoke her mind, she'd be speechless.

She thought she could only use her AM radio in the morning.

She had a shirt that said "TGIF," which she thought stood for "This Goes In Front"

Maybe she was blonde?

※ ※ ※

Blind Man

Two nuns are ordered to paint a room in the convent which is being renovated, and the last instruction of the Mother Superior is that they must not get even a drop of paint on their habits.

After conferring about this for a while, the two nuns decide to lock the door of the room, strip off their habits, and paint in the nude.

In the middle of the project, there comes a knock at the door.

"Who is it?" calls one of the nuns.

"Blind man," replies a voice from the other side of the door.

The two nuns look at each other, shrug, and decide that no harm can come from letting a blind man into the room. They open the door, and a man enters.

"Nice boobs," says the man. "Where do you want these blinds?"

❋❋❋

CATHOLIC HORSES

Bubba was from Alabama and was, a hard-shell Southern Baptist. He loved to sneak away to the race track. One day he was there betting on the ponies and losing his shirt when he noticed a priest step out onto the track and bless the forehead of one of the horses lining up for the 4th race. Lo and behold, this horse – a very long shot—won the race.

Bubba was most interested to see what the priest did in the next race. Sure enough, he watched the priest step out onto the track as the horses for the fifth race lined up, and placed a blessing on the forehead of one of the horses. Bubba made a beeline for the window and placed a small bet on the horse.

Again, even though another long shot, the horse the priest had blessed won the race. Bubba collected his winning and anxiously waited to see which horse the priest bestowed his blessing on for the 6th race.

The priest showed, blessed a horse, Bubba bet on it, and it won! Bubba was elated!

As the day went on, the priest continued blessing one of the horses, and it always came in first. Bubba began to pull in some serious money, and by the last race, he knew his wildest dreams were going to come true.

Entertaining!
Amazing!

He made a quick stop at the ATM, withdrew big money and awaited the priest's blessing that would tell him which horse to bet on.

True to his pattern, the priest stepped out onto the track before the last race and blessed the forehead, eyes, ears and hooves of one of the horses.

Bubba bet every cent, and watched the horse come in dead last. He was dumbfounded. He made his way to the track and when he found the priest, he demanded, "What happened, Father? All day you blessed horses and they won. The last race, you blessed a horse and he lost. Now I've lost my savings, thanks to you!!"

The priest nodded wisely and said, "That's the problem with you Protestants…you can't tell the difference between a simple blessing and the Last Rites."

☀ ☀ ☀

God, grant me the serenity to accept the things I cannot change,
The courage to change the things I cannot accept,
And the wisdom to hide the bodies of those people I had to kill today because they pissed me off.
And also help me to be careful of the toes I step on today,
As they may be connected to the ass I have to kiss tomorrow.
Help me to always give 100% at work…
12% on Mondays, 23% on Tuesdays, 47% on Wednesdays, 16% on Thursdays, and 2% on Fridays.
And help me to remember that when I'm having a really bad day,
And it seems people are trying to upset me,
That it takes 42 muscles to frown
And only 4 to extend my middle finger and tell them to bite me.
And help me to remember that stressed is desserts spelled backwards.

64

Exciting!
Emotional!

Chapter 2. Animal. Blonde. Church Humor

✳✳✳

"Bless me Father, for I have sinned. I have been with a loose woman."

The priest asks, "Is that you, little Tommy Shaughnessy?"

"Yes, Father, it is."

"And, who was the woman you were with?"

"Sure and I can't be tellin' you, Father. I don't want to ruin her reputation."

"Well, Tommy, I'm sure to find out sooner or later, so you may as well tell me now. Was it Brenda O'Malley?"

"I cannot say."

"Was it Patricia Kelly?"

"I'll never tell."

"Was it Liz Shannon?"

"I'm sorry, but I can't name her."

"Was it Cathy Morgan?"

"My lips are sealed."

"Was it Fiona McDonald, then?"

"Please, Father, I cannot tell you."

The priest sighs in frustration. "You're a steadfast lad, Tommy Shaughnessy, and I admire that. But you've sinned, and you must atone. You cannot attend church for three months. Be off with you now."

Tommy walks back to his pew. His friend Sean slides over and whispers, "What'd you get?"

"Three month's vacation and five good leads," says Tommy.

✳✳✳

Entertaining!
Amazing!

Sister Mary Holycard was in her 60s, and much admired for her sweetness and kindness to all.

One afternoon early in the spring a young priest came to chat, so she welcomed him into her Victorian parlor. She then invited him to have a seat while she prepared a little tea.

As he sat facing her old pump organ, the young priest noticed a crystal glass bowl sitting on top of it filled with water, and in the water floated, a condom.

Well, imagine how shocked and surprised he was.

Imagine his curiosity!

Surely, he thought, Sister Mary has flipped or something!

When she returned with tea and cookies, they began to chat.

The priest tried to stifle his curiosity about the bowl of water and the condom floater but soon it got the better of him.

He could resist no longer. "Sister," he asked, "I wonder if you could tell me about this?" (pointing at the crystal bowl).

"Oh, yes," she replied, "isn't it wonderful? I was walking downtown last fall and I found this little package. The directions said to put it on the organ, keep it wet, and it would prevent disease, and you know, I haven't had a cold all winter!"

❊❊❊

A man is driving down a deserted stretch of highway when he notices a sign out of the corner of his eye. It reads SISTERS OF ST. FRANCIS HOUSE OF PROSTITUTION 10 MILES he thinks it was just a figment of his imagination and drives on without a second thought.

Soon he sees another sign which says SISTERS OF ST. FRANCIS HOUSE OF PROSTITUTION 5 MILES.

Exciting!
Emotional!

Suddenly, he begins to realize that these signs are for real. Then he drives past a third sign saying SISTERS OF ST. FRANCIS HOUSE OF PROSTITUTION NEXT RIGHT.

His curiosity gets the best of him and he pulls into the drive. On the far side of the parking lot is a somber stone building with a small sign next to the door reading SISTERS OF ST. FRANCIS HOUSE OF PROSTITUTION.

He climbs the steps and rings the bell. The door is answered by a nun in a long black habit who asks, "What may we do for you, my son?"

He answers, "I saw your signs along the highway, and was interested in possibly doing business."

"Very well, my son, please follow me."

He is led through many winding passages and is soon quite disoriented.

The nun stops at a closed door, and tells the man, "Please knock on this door."

He does as he is told and another nun in a long habit, holding a tin cup, answers this door. This nun instructs, "Please place $50 in the cup, then go through the large wooden door at the end of this hallway."

He gets $50 out of his wallet and places it in the second nun's cup. He trots eagerly down the hall and slips through the door, pulling it shut behind him.

As the door locks behind him, he finds himself back in the parking lot, facing another small sign:

GO IN PEACE. YOU HAVE JUST BEEN SCREWED BY THE SISTERS OF ST. FRANCIS.

☀☀☀

Entertaining!
Amazing!

Forgiving your enemies

The preacher, in his Sunday sermon, used "Forgive Your Enemies" as his subject. After a long sermon, he asked how many were willing to forgive their enemies.

About half held up their hands.

Not satisfied he harangued for another twenty minutes and repeated his question. This time he received a response of about 80 percent.

Still unsatisfied, he lectured for another 15 minutes and repeated his question. With all thoughts now on Sunday dinner, all responded except one elderly lady in the rear.

"Mrs. Jones, are you not willing to forgive your enemies?"

"I don't have any."

"Mrs. Jones, that is very unusual. How old are you?"

"Ninety-three."

"Mrs. Jones, please come down in front and tell the congregation how a person can live to be ninety-three, and not have an enemy in the world."

The little sweetheart of a lady tottered down the aisle, very slowly turned around and said: "It's easy, I just outlived the bitches."

☀☀☀

Thank God for church ladies with typewriters. These sentences actually appeared in church bulletins or were announced in church services:

1. Bertha Belch, a missionary from Africa, will be speaking tonight at Calvary Methodist. Come hear Bertha Belch all the way from Africa.

2. Announcement in a church bulletin for a national PRAYER AND FASTING Conference: "The cost for attending the Fasting and Prayer conference includes meals."

3. The sermon this morning: "Jesus Walks on the Water." The sermon tonight: "Searching for Jesus."

4. Our youth basketball team is back in action Wednesday at 8 PM in the recreation hall. Come out and watch us kill Christ the King.

5. "Ladies, don't forget the rummage sale. It's a chance to get rid of those things not worth keeping around the house. Don't forget your husbands."

6. The peacemaking meeting scheduled for today has been cancelled due to a conflict.

7. Remember in prayer the many who are sick of our community.

8. Smile at someone who is hard to love. Say "hell" to someone who doesn't care much about you.

9. Don't let worry kill you off – let the Church help.

10. Miss Charlene Mason sang "I will not pass this way again," giving obvious pleasure to the congregation.

11. For those of you who have children and don't know it, we have a nursery downstairs.

12. Next Thursday there will be tryouts for the choir. They need all the help they can get.

13. Barbara remains in the hospital and needs blood donors for more transfusions. She is also having trouble sleeping and requests tapes of Pastor Jack's sermons.

Entertaining!
Amazing!

14. During the absence of our Pastor, we enjoyed the rare privilege of hearing a good sermon when J.F. Stubbs supplied our pulpit.

15. Irving Benson and Jessie Carter were married on October 24 in the church. So ends a friendship that began in their school days.

16. At the evening service tonight, the sermon topic will be "What is Hell?" Come early and listen to our choir practice.

17. Eight new choir robes are currently needed, due to the addition of several new members and to the deterioration of some older ones.

18. Scouts are saving aluminium cans, bottles, and other items to be recycled. Proceeds will be used to cripple children.

19. The Lutheran men's group will meet at 6 PM. Steak, mashed potatoes, green beans, bread and dessert will be served for a nominal feel.

20. Please place your donation in the envelope along with the deceased person you want remembered.

21. Attend and you will hear an excellent speaker and heave a healthy lunch.

22. The church will host an evening of fine dining, superb entertainment, and gracious hostility.

23. Potluck supper Sunday at 5:00 PM—prayer and medication to follow.

24. The ladies of the Church have cast off clothing of every kind. They may be seen in the basement on Friday afternoon.

Exciting!
Emotional!

25. This evening at 7 PM there will be a hymn sing in the park across from the Church. Bring a blanket and come prepared to sin.

26. Ladies Bible Study will be held Thursday morning at 10. All ladies are invited to lunch in the Fellowship Hall after the B.S. is done.

27. The pastor would appreciate it if the ladies of the congregation would lend him their electric girdles for the pancake breakfast next Sunday.

28. Low Self Esteem Support Group will meet Thursday at 7 PM. Please use the back door.

29. The eighth-graders will be presenting Shakespeare's Hamlet in the Church basement Friday at 7 PM. The Congregation is invited to attend this tragedy.

30. Weight Watchers will meet at 7 PM at the First Presbyterian Church. Please use large double door at the side entrance.

❀❀❀

The Golfing Nun

A nun is sitting with her Mother Superior chatting. "I used some horrible language this week and feel absolutely terrible about it."

"When did you use this awful language?" asks the elder.

"Well, I was golfing and hit an incredible drive that looked like it was going to go over 250 yards, but it struck a phone line that was hanging over the fairway and fell straight down to the ground after going only about 75 yards."

"Is THAT when you swore?"

71

Entertaining!
Amazing!

"No, Mother," says the nun. "After that, a squirrel ran out of the bushes and grabbed my ball in its mouth and began to run away."

"Is THAT when you swore?" asks the Mother Superior again. "Well, no." says the nun. "You see, as the squirrel was running, an eagle came down out of the sky, grabbed the squirrel in his talons and began to fly away!"

"Is THAT when you swore?" asks the amazed elder nun.

"No, not yet. As the eagle carried the squirrel away in its claws, it flew near the green and the squirrel dropped my ball."

"Did you swear THEN?" asked Mother Superior, becoming impatient. "No, because the ball fell on a big rock, bounced over the sandtrap, rolled onto the green, and stopped about six inches from the hole."

The two nuns were silent for a moment.

Then Mother Superior sighed and said, "You missed the f**cking putt, didn't you?"

❋❋❋

A funny one for Monday

An Irishman with a bad leg hobbled into a restaurant one afternoon.
He painfully sat down at a booth and asked the waitress for a cup of coffee.
The Irishman looked across the restaurant and asked, "Is that Jesus over there?"
The waitress nodded so the Irishman told her to give Jesus a cup of coffee, too.
The next patron to come in was an Englishman with a hunched back.
He shuffled over to a booth and asked the waitress for a glass of hot tea.
He also glanced across the restaurant and asked "Is that Jesus over there?"
The waitress nodded so the Englishman said to give Jesus a cup of hot tea, too.
The third patron to come into the restaurant was an Alabama Redneck.

72

He swaggered over to a booth, sat down and hollered "Hey there sweet thang, hows about gettin' me a cold glass of Coke!" He, too, looked across the restaurant and asked "Is that God's boy over there?"

The waitress nodded so the Redneck said to give Jesus a cold glass of coke, too.

As Jesus got up to leave, He passed by the Irishman and touched him and said "For your kindness, you are healed. The Irishman felt the strength come back into his leg and got up and danced a jig out the door.

Jesus also passed by the Englishman, touched him and said, "For your kindness, you are healed."

The Englishman felt his back straightening up and he raised up his hands, praised the Lord and did a series of back flips out the door.

Then Jesus walked towards the Redneck. The Redneck jumps up and yells, "Hey man don't touch me…I'm drawin' disability!!!!!"

❋ ❋ ❋

Catholic School

Kids were lined up in the cafeteria of a Catholic school for lunch.

At the head of the table was a large pile of apples. The nun had written a note: "Take only one, God is watching."

Moving through the line to the other end of the table, the children found a large pile of chocolate chip cookies.

A little boy wrote a note and put it on the cookies: "Take all you want – God is watching the apples!"

Entertaining!
Amazing!

※ ※ ※

An engineer of the Harley Davidson Motorcycle Corporation died and went to heaven. At the gates, St. Peter told him, "Since you've been such a good man and your motorcycles have changed the world, your reward is you can hang out with anyone you want in Heaven." The Engineer thought about it for a minute and then said, "I want to hang out with God." St. Peter took him to the Throne Room, and introduced him to God. The engineer then asked God, "Hey, aren't you the inventor of Woman?" God said, "Ah, yes." "Well," said the engineer, "professional to professional, you have some major design flaws in your invention."

1. There's too much inconsistency in the front-end protrusion.
2. It chatters constantly at high speeds.
3. Most of the rear ends are too soft and wobble too much.
4. The intake is placed way too close to the exhaust.
5. And finally, the maintenance costs are outrageous."

"Hmmmm, you may have some good points there," replied God, "hold on."

God went to his Celestial super computer, typed in a few words and waited for the results. The computer printed out a slip of paper and God read it.

"Well, it may be true that my invention is flawed," God said to the engineer, "but according to these numbers, more men are riding my invention than yours."

※ ※ ※

Exciting!
Emotional!

Love how kids see things.

A little boy wanted $100.00 very badly and prayed for weeks, but nothing happened. Then he decided to write God a letter requesting the $100.00.

When the postal authorities received the letter to God, USA, they decided to send it to the President. The president was so amused that he instructed his secretary to send the little boy a $5.00 bill. The president thought this would appear to be a lot of money to a little boy.

The little boy was delighted with the $5.00 bill and sat down to write a thank-you note to God, which read:

Dear God:

Thank you very much for sending the money. However, I noticed that for some reason you sent it through Washington, DC, and those assholes deducted $95.00 in taxes.

❀❀❀

- One Sunday in a Midwest City, a young child was "acting up" during the morning worship hour. The parents did their best to maintain some sense of order in the pew but were losing the battle. Finally, the father picked the little fellow up and walked sternly up the aisle on his way out. Just before reaching the safety of the foyer, the little one called loudly to the congregation, "Pray for me! Pray for me!

- A little boy was overheard praying: "Lord, if you can't make me a better boy, don't worry about it. I'm having a real good time like I am."

75

Entertaining!
Amazing!

- A Sunday school teacher asked her little children, as they were on the way to church service, "And why is it necessary to be quiet in church?" One bright little girl replied, "Because people are sleeping."

✵ ✵ ✵

AND you wanna have kids...

After creating heaven and earth, God created Adam and Eve. And the first thing he said was, "Don't." "Don't what?" Adam replied. "Don't eat the forbidden fruit."

God said. "Forbidden fruit? We have forbidden fruit?

Hey, Eve...we have forbidden fruit!" "No way!"

"Yes, way!"

"Do NOT eat the fruit!" said God. "Why?" "Because I am your Father and I said so!" God replied, (wondering why he hadn't stopped creation after making the elephants). A few minutes later, God saw His children having a forbidden fruit break and was He ticked!

"Didn't I tell you not to eat the fruit?" God, as our first parent, asked, "Uh huh," Adam replied. "Then why did you?" said the Father. "I don't know," said Eve.

"She started it!" Adam said, "Did not!" "Did, too!"

"DID NOT! Having had it with the two of them, God's punishment was that Adam and Eve should have children of their own. Thus, the pattern was set and it has never changed!

But there is reassurance in this story. If you have persistently and lovingly tried to give children wisdom and they haven't taken it, don't be hard on yourself. If God had trouble raising children, what makes you think it would be a piece of cake for you?

76

Children

– Advice for the day: If you have a lot of tension and you get a headache, do what it says on the aspirin bottle: "Take two Aspirin" and "Keep away from children."

– You spend the first 2 years of their life teaching them to walk and talk. Then you spend the next 16 telling them to sit down and shut-up.

– Grandchildren are God's reward for not killing your children.

– Mothers of teens know why some animals eat their young.

– Children seldom misquote you. In fact, they usually repeat word for word what you shouldn't have said.

– The main purpose of holding children's parties is to remind yourself that there are children more awful than your own.

– We childproofed our home three years ago and they're still getting in!

– Be nice to your kids. They'll choose your nursing home.

❂❂❂

And the Lord spoke to Noah and said,

"In one year, I am going to make it rain and cover the whole Earth with water until all flesh is destroyed. But I want you to save the righteous people and two of every kind of living thing on the earth. therefore, I am commanding you to build an Ark."

In a flash of lightning, God delivered the specifications for an Ark.

In fear and trembling, Noah took the plans and agreed to build the Ark.

77

Entertaining!
Emazing!

"Remember" said the Lord, "You must complete the Ark and bring everything aboard in one year."

Exactly one year later, fierce storm clouds covered the earth and all the seas of the earth went into a tumult.

The Lord saw that Noah was sitting in his front yard weeping.

"Noah," He shouted. "Where is the Ark?"

"Lord, please forgive me!" cried Noah. "I did my best, but there were big problems. First, I had to get a permit for construction and your plans did not meet the codes. I had to hire an engineering firm and redraw the plans. Then I got into a fight with OSHA over whether or not the Ark needed a fire sprinkler system and flotation devices.

"Then my neighbor objected, claiming I was violating zoning ordinances by building the Ark in my front yard, so I had to get a variance from the city planning commission.

"Then I had problems getting enough wood for the Ark, because there was a ban on cutting trees to protect the Spotted Owl. I finally convinced the U.S. Forest Service that I needed the wood to save the owls. However, the Fish and Wildlife Service won't let me catch any owls. So, no owls.

"The carpenters formed a union and went out on strike. I had to negotiate a settlement with the National Labor Relations Board before anyone would pick up a saw or a hammer. Now I have 16 carpenters on the Ark, but still no owls.

"When I started rounding up the other animals, I got sued by an animal rights group. They objected to me only taking two of each kind aboard. Just when I got the suit dismissed, the EPA notified me that I could not complete the Ark without filing an environmental impact statement on your proposed flood. They didn't take very kindly to the idea that they had no jurisdiction over the conduct of the Creator of the universe.

Exciting!
Emotional!

"Then the Army Engineers demanded a map of the proposed new flood plan. I sent them a map.

"Right now, I am trying to resolve a complaint filed with the Equal Employment Opportunity Commission that I am practicing discrimination by not taking godless, unbelieving people aboard.

"The IRS has seized my assets, claiming that I'm building the Ark in preparation to flee the country to avoid paying taxes.

"I just got a notice from the state that I owe them some kind of user tax and failed to register the Ark as a "recreational watercraft."

"Finally, the ACLU got the courts to issue an injunction against further construction of the Ark, saying that since God is flooding the earth, it is a religious event and therefore unconstitutional. I really don't think I can finish the Ark for another five or six years!" Noah wailed.

The sky began to clear, the sun began to shine and the seas began to calm. A rainbow arched across the sky.

Noah looked up hopefully. "You mean You are not going to destroy the earth, Lord?"

"No," said the Lord sadly. "I don't have to. The government already has."

Entertaining!
Amazing!

World's Funniest and Greatest E-mails

Chapter 3

Inspirational

Love starts with a smile, grows with a kiss, and ends with a tear.

Don't cry over anyone who won't cry over you.

If love isn't a game, why are there so many players?

Good friends are hard to find, harder to leave, and impossible to forget.

You can only go as far as you push.

Actions speak louder than words.

The hardest thing to do is watch the one you love, love somebody else.

Don't let the past hold you back; you're missing the good stuff.

Life's short. If you don't look around once in a while you might miss it.

A BEST FRIEND is like a four leaf clover, HARD TO FIND and LUCKY TO HAVE.

Some people make the world SPECIAL just by being in it.

BEST FRIENDS are the siblings God forgot to give us.

When it hurts to look back, and you're scared to look ahead, you can look beside you and your BEST FRIEND will be there.

TRUE FRIENDSHIP "NEVER" ENDS. Friends are FOREVER.

Good friends are like stars…You don't always see them, but you know they are always there.

Don't frown. You never know who is falling in love with your smile.

What do you do when the only person who can make you stop crying is the person who made you cry?

Nobody is perfect until you fall in love with them.

Everything is okay in the end. If it's not okay, then it's not the end.

Most people walk in and out of you life, only friends leave footprints in your heart.

❀❀❀

A woman came out of her house and saw three old men with long white beards sitting in her front yard. She did not recognize them. She said "I don't think I know you, but you must be hungry. Please come in and have something to eat."

"Is the man of the house home?", they asked.

"No", she replied. "He's out."

"Then we cannot come in", they replied.

In the evening when her husband came home, she told him what had happened.

"Go tell them I am home and invite them in!"

The woman went out and invited the men in.

"We do not go into a House together," they replied.

"Why is that?" she asked.

One of the old men explained: "His name is Wealth," he said pointing to one of his friends, and said pointing to another one, "He is Success, and I am Love." Then he added, "Now go in and discuss with your husband which one of us you want in your home."

The woman went in and told her husband what was said. Her husband was overjoyed. "How nice!!", he said. "Since that is the case, let us invite Wealth. Let him come and fill our home with wealth!"

His wife disagreed. "My dear, why don't we invite Success?"

Their daughter-in-law was listening from the other corner of the house. She jumped in with her own suggestion: "Would it not be better to invite Love? Our home will then be filled with love!"

"Let us heed our daughter-in-law's advice," said the husband to his wife.

"Go out and invite Love to be our guest."

The woman went out and asked the three old men, "Which one of you is Love? Please come in and be our guest."

Entertaining!
Amazing!

Love got up and started walking toward the house. The other two also got up and followed him. Surprised, the lady asked Wealth and Success: "I only invited Love, Why are you coming in?"

The old men replied together: "If you had invited Wealth or Success, the other two of us would've stayed out, but since you invited Love, wherever He goes, we go with him. Wherever there is Love, there is also Wealth and Success!!!!!!"

※※※

My Wish For You...

- Where there is pain, I wish you peace and mercy.
- Where there is self-doubting, I wish you a renewed confidence in your ability to work through it.
- Where there is tiredness, or exhaustion, I wish you understanding, patience, and renewed strength.
- Where there is fear, I wish you love and courage.

You have two choices right now:
1. Click this off
2. Invite love by sharing this story with all the people you care about.

I hope you will choose #2. I did.

※※※

84

Exciting!
Emotional!

What is a grandmother? (taken from papers written by a class of 8-year olds)

A grandmother is a lady who has no little children of her own. She likes other people's.

A grandfather is a man grandmother.

Grandmothers don't have to do anything except be there when we come to see them. They are so old they shouldn't play hard or run. It is good if they drive us to the store and have lots of quarters for us.

When they take us for walks, they slow down past things like pretty leaves and caterpillars.

They show us and talk to us about the color of the flowers and also why we shouldn't step on "cracks."

They don't say, "Hurry up."

Usually grandmothers are fat, but not too fat to tie your shoes.

They wear glasses and funny underwear.

They can take their teeth and gums out.

Grandmothers don't have to be smart.

They have to answer questions like "why isn't God married?" and "How come dogs chase cats?".

When they read to us, they don't skip. They don't mind if we ask for the same story over again.

85

Entertaining!
Amazing!

Everybody should try to have a grandmother, especially if you don't have television, because they are the only grown ups who like to spend time with us.

They know we should have snack-time before bedtime and they say prayers with us every time, and kiss us even when we've acted bad.

※ ※ ※

Trucker's Story

No joke this morning, just a really touching story. I got this from a friend who passed it on from a friend.

If this doesn't light your fire – your wood is wet!!

I try not to be biased but I had my doubts about hiring Stevie. His placement counselor assured me that he would be a good, reliable busboy.

But I had never had a mentally handicapped employee and wasn't sure I wanted one. I wasn't sure how my customers would react to Stevie. He was short, a little dumpy with the smooth facial features and the thick-tongued speech of Down Syndrome. I wasn't worried about most of my trucker customers because truckers don't generally care who buses tables as long as the meatloaf platter is good and the pies are homemade. The four-wheel drivers were the ones who concerned me; the mouthy college kids traveling to school; the yuppie snobs who secretly polish their silverware with their napkins for fear of catching some dreaded "truck stop germ"; the pairs of white shirted business men on expense accounts who think every truck stop waitress wants to be flirted with. So I watched Stevie closley for the first few weeks. I shouldn't have worried.

After the first week, Stevie had the staff wrapped around his stubby little finger, and within a month my truck regulars had adopted him as their official truck stop mascot. After that, I really didn't care what the rest of the customers

86

Exciting!
Emotional!

thought of him. He was like a 21-year old in blue jeans and Nikes, eager to laugh and eager to please, but fierce in his attention to his duties. Every salt and pepper shaker was exactly in its place, not a bread crumb or coffee spill was visible when Stevie got done with each table.

Our only problem was persuading him to wait to clean a table until after the customers were finished. He would hover in the background, shifting his weight from one foot to the other, scanning the dining room until a table was empty. Then he would scurry to the empty table and carefully bus dishes and glasses onto the cart and meticulously wipe the table up with a practiced flourish of his rag. If he thought a customer was watching, his brow would pucker with added concentration. He took pride in doing his job exactly right, and you had to love how hard he tried to please each and every person he met.

Over time, we learned that he lived with his mother, a widow who was disabled after repeated surgeries for cancer. They lived on their Social Security benefits in public housing two miles from the truck stop.

Their social worker, who stopped to check on him every so often, admitted they had fallen between the cracks. Money was tight, and what I paid him was probably the difference between them being able to live together and Stevie being sent to a group home. That's why the restaurant was a gloomy place that morning last August, the first morning in three years that Stevie missed work. He was at the Mayo Clinic in Rochester getting a new valve or something put in his heart. His social worker said that people with Down syndrome often had heart problems at an early age so this wasn't unexpected, and there was a good chance he would come through the surgery in good shape and be back at work in a few months. A ripple of excitement ran through the staff later that morning when word came that Stevie was out of surgery, in recovery and doing fine. Frannie, head waitress, let out a war

Entertaining!
Amazing!

hoop and did a little dance in the aisle when she heard the good news. Bell Ringer, one of our regular trucker customers, stared at the sight of the 50-year-old grandmother of four doing a victory shimmy beside his table. Frannie blushed, smoothed her apron and shot Bell Ringer a withering look. He grinned. "OK, Frannie, what was that all about?" he asked. "We just got word that Stevie is out of surgery and going to be okay." "I was wondering where he was. I had a new joke to tell him. What was the surgery about?"

Frannie quickly told Bell Ringer and the other two drivers sitting at his booth about Stevie's surgery, then sighed. "Yeah, I'm glad he is going to be OK" she said. "But I don't know how he and his Mom are going to handle all the bills. From what I hear, they're barely getting by as it is."

Bell Ringer nodded thoughtfully, and Frannie hurried off to wait on the rest of her tables. Since I hadn't had time to round up a busboy to replace Stevie and really didn't want to replace him, the girls were busing their own tables that day until we decided what to do.

After the morning rush, Frannie walked into my office. She had a couple of paper napkins in her hand a funny look on her face. "What's up?" I asked.

"I didn't get that table where Bell Ringer and his friends were sitting cleared off. After they left Pony Pete and Tony Tipper were sitting there when I got back to clean it off," she said. "This was folded and tucked under a coffee cup." She handed the napkin to me, and three $20 bills fell onto my desk when I opened it. On the outside, in big, bold letters, was printed "Something For Stevie." "Pony Pete asked me what that was all about," she said, "so I told about Stevie and his Mom and everything, and Pete looked at Tony and Tony looked at Pete, and they ended up giving me this." She handed me another paper napkin that had "Something For Stevie"

Exciting!
Emotional!

scrawled on its outside. Two $50 bills were tucked within its folds. Frannie looked at me with wet, shiny eyes, shook her head and said simply "truckers."

That was three months ago. Today is Thanksgiving, the first day Stevie is supposed to be back to work. His placement worker said he's been counting the days until the doctor said he could work, and it didn't matter at all that it was a holiday. He called 10 times in the past week, making sure we knew he was coming, fearful that we had forgotten him or that his job was in jeopardy. I arranged to have his mother bring him to work, met them in the parking lot and invited them both to celebrate his day back. Stevie was thinner and paler, but couldn't stop grinning as he pushed through the doors and headed for the back room where his apron and busing cart were waiting.

"Hold up there, Stevie, not so fast," I said. I took him and his mother by their arms. "Work can wait for a minute. To celebrate you coming back, breakfast for you and your mother is on me!" I led them toward a large corner booth at the rear of the room. I could feel and hear the rest of the staff following behind as we marched through the dining room. Glancing over my shoulder, I saw booth after booth of grinning truckers empty and join the procession. We stopped in front of the big table. Its surface was covered with coffee cups, saucers and dinner plates, all sitting slightly crooked on dozens of folded paper napkins. "First thing you have to do, Stevie, is clean up this mess," I said. I tried to sound stern. Stevie looked at me, and then at his mother, then pulled out one of the napkins. It had "Something for Stevie" printed on the outside. As he picked it up, two $10 bills fell onto the table. Stevie stared at the money, then at all the napkins peeking from beneath the table-ware, each with his name printed or scrawled on it. I turned to his mother. "There's more than $10,000 in cash and checks on that table, all from truckers and trucking companies that heard about your problems. "Happy Thanksgiving!"

Well, it got real noisy about that time, with everybody hollering and shouting, and there were a few tears as well. But you know what's funny? While everybody else was busy shaking hands and hugging each other, Stevie, with a big, big smile on his face, was busy clearing all the cups and dishes from the table.

Best worker I ever hired.

Plant a seed and watch it grow. At this point, you can bury this inspirational message or forward it fulfilling the need! If you shed a tear, hug yourself because you are a compassionate person.

WELL...DON'T JUST SIT THERE SEND THIS STORY ON! When you're lonely, I wish you LOVE. When you're down, I wish you JOY. When things get complicated, I wish you FAITH.

When things look empty, I wish you HOPE.

☀ ☀ ☀

An Old Lady's Poem

When an old lady died in the geriatric ward of a small hospital near Dundee, Scotland, it was felt that she had nothing left of any value.

Later, when the nurses were going through her meager possessions, they found this poem.

It's quality and content so impressed the staff that copies were made and distributed to every nurse in the hospital. One nurse took her copy to Ireland. The old lady's sole bequest to posterity has since appeared in the Christmas Edition of the News Magazine of the North Ireland Association for Mental Health. A slide presentation has also been made based on her simple, but eloquent, poem....And

Exciting!
Emotional!

this little old Scottish lady, with nothing left to give to the world, is now the author of this "anonymous" poem winging across the Internet. Goes to show that we all leave "SOME footprints in time"…

An Old Lady's Poem

What do you see, nurses, what do you see?
What are you thinking when you're looking at me?
A crabby old woman, not very wise,
Uncertain of habit, with faraway eyes?

Who dribbles her food and makes no reply.
When you say in a loud voice, "I do wish you'd try!"
Who seems not to notice the things that you do,
And forever is losing a stocking or shoe…

Who, resisting or not, lets you do as you will,
With bathing and feeding, the long day to fill…
Is that what you're thinking? Is that what you see?
Then open your eyes, nurse, you're not looking at me.

I'll tell you who I am as I sit here so still,
As I do at your bidding, as I eat at your will.
I'm a small child of ten…with a father and mother,
Brothers and sisters, who love one another.

A young girl of sixteen, with wings on her feet,
Dreaming that soon now a lover she'll meet.
A bride soon at twenty – my heart gives a leap,
Remembering the vows that I promised to keep.

At twenty-five now, I have young of my own,
Who need me to guide and a secure happy home.
A woman of thirty, my young now grown fast,
Bound to each other with ties that should last.

At forty, my young sons have grown and are gone,
But my man's beside me to see I don't mourn.
At fifty once more, babies play round my knee,
Again we know children, my loved one and me.

Dark days are upon me, my husband is dead;
I look at the future, I shudder with dread.
For my young are all rearing young of their own,
And I think of the years and the love that I've known.

I'm now an old woman…and nature is cruel;
'Tis jest to make old age look like a fool.
The body, it crumbles, grace and vigor depart,
There is now a stone where I once had a heart.

exciting!
emotional!

But inside this old carcass a young girl still dwells,
And now and again my battered heart swells.
I remember the joys, I remember the pain,
And I'm loving and living life over again.

I think of the years all too few, gone too fast,
And accept the stark fact that nothing can last.
So open your eyes, nurses, open and see,...
Not a crabby old woman; look closer, see ME!!

Remember this poem when you next meet an old person who you might brush aside without looking at the young soul within. We will one day be there, too!

✷✷✷

15 Things You Probably Never Knew or Thought About:

1. At least five people in this world love you so much they would die for you.
2. At least fifteen people in this world love you in some way.
3. The only reason anyone would ever hate you is because they want to be just like you.
4. A smile from you can bring happiness to anyone, even if they don't like you.
5. Every night, SOMEONE thinks about you before they go to sleep.
6. You mean the world to someone.
7. If not for you, someone may not be living.
8. You are special and unique.
9. Someone that you don't even know exists loves you.

Entertaining!
Amazing!

10. When you make the biggest mistake ever, something good comes from it.

11. When you think the world has turned its back on you, take a look: you most likely turned your back on the world.

12. When you think you have no chance of getting what you want, you probably won't get it; however if you believe in yourself, probably, sooner or later, you will get it.

13. Always remember the compliments you received. Forget about the rude remarks.

14. Always tell someone how you feel about them; you will feel much better when they know.

15. If you have a great friend, take the time to let them know that they are great.

Send this to people you care about, including the person who sent this to you. If you do so, you will certainly brighten someone's day and might change his or her perspective on life for the better.

☀☀☀

Pay attention to what you read. After you read this you will know the reason it was sent to you.

People come into your life for a reason, a season or a lifetime. When you figure out which one it is, you will know what to do with each person.

When someone comes into your life for a REASON it is usually to meet a need you have expressed. They come to assist you through a difficulty, to provide you with guidance and support, to aid you physically, emotionally or spiritually. They may seem like a godsend, and they are.

94

Exciting!
Emotional!

They are there for a reason you need them to be. Then, without any wrong doing on your part, or at an inconvenient time, this person will say or do something to bring the relationship to an end.

Sometimes they die. Sometimes they walk away. Sometimes they act up and force you to take a stand.

What we must realize is that our need has been met, our desire fulfilled, their work is done.

The prayer you sent up has been answered. And now it is time to move on.

When people come into your life for a SEASON it is because your turn has come to share, grow or learn. They bring you an experience of peace or make you laugh. They may teach you something you have never done. They usually give you an unbelievable amount of joy. Believe it! It is real! But, only for a season.

LIFETIME relationships teach you lifetime lessons, things you must build upon in order to have a solid emotional foundation. Your job is to accept the lesson, love the person, and put what you have learned to use in all other areas of your life. It is said that love is blind but friendship is clairvoyant.

Thank you for being a part of my life.

Work like you don't need the money,
Love like you've never been hurt,
And dance like no one is watching!

※ ※ ※

Entertaining!
Amazing!

World's Funniest and Greatest E-mails

Imagine…

There is a bank that credits your account each morning with $86,400.

It carries over no balance from day to day.

Every evening deletes whatever part of the balance you failed to use during the day. What would you do? Draw out ALL OF IT, of course!!!!

Each of us has such a bank. Its name is TIME.

Every morning it credits you with 86,400 seconds. Every night it writes off, as lost, whatever of this you have failed to invest to good purpose. It carries over no balance. It allows no overdraft.

Each day it opens a new account for you.

Each night it burns the remains of the day.

If you fail to use the day's deposits, the loss is yours.

There is no going back. There is no drawing against the "tomorrow."

You must live in the present on today's deposits. Invest it so as to get from it the utmost in health, happiness and success!

The clock is running. Make the most of today.

To realize the value of ONE YEAR,
ask a student who failed a grade.

To realize the value of ONE MONTH,
ask a mother who gave birth to a premature baby.

To realize the value of ONE WEEK,
ask the editor of a weekly newspaper.

To realize the value of ONE HOUR,
ask the lovers who are waiting to meet.

To realize the value of ONE MINUTE,
ask a person who missed the train.

To realize the value of ONE-SECOND,
ask a person who just avoided an accident.

To realize the value of ONE MILLISECOND,
ask the person who won a silver medal in the Olympics.

Treasure every moment that you have! And treasure it more because you shared it with someone special, special enough to spend your time.

And remember that time waits for no one.

Yesterday is history. Tomorrow is a mystery. Today is a gift. That's why it's called the "present"!!!

✸✸✸

Friends are a very rare jewel, indeed.

They make you smile and encourage you to succeed. They lend an ear, they share a word of praise, and they always want to open their heart to us.

Send this to everyone you consider a FRIEND.

If it comes back to you, then you'll know you have a circle of friends.

Entertaining!
Amazing!

✹ ✹ ✹

A Reminder To Be Thankful

I am thankful...

For the wife who says it's hot dogs tonight. She is home with me, not with someone else.

For the husband who is on the sofa who is being a couch potato. He is home with me and not out at the bars.

For the teenager who is complaining about doing dishes, because that means she is at home, not on the streets.

For the taxes that I pay, because it means that I am employed.

For the mess to clean after a party, because it means that I have been surrounded by friends.

For the clothes that fit a little too snug, because it means I have enough to eat.

For my shadow that watches me work, because it means I am out in the sunshine.

For a lawn that needs mowing, windows that need cleaning and gutters that need fixing, because it means I have a home.

For all the complaining I hear about the government, because it means that we have freedom of speech.

For the parking spot I find at the far end of the parking lot, because it means I am capable of walking and that I have been blessed with transportation.

98

For the lady behind me in church that sings off key, because it means that I can hear.

For the pile of laundry and ironing, because it means I have clothes to wear.

For weariness and aching muscles at the end of the day, because it means I am capable of working hard.

For the alarm that goes off in the early morning hours, because it means that I am alive.

And finally…for too much e-mail, because it means I have friends who are thinking of me.

Send this to those you care about…I just did.

☀☀☀

Enjoy – Very Uplifting

Make sure you read all the way down to the last sentence, and don't skip ahead.

I've learned…
That life is like a roll of toilet paper. The closer it gets to the end, the faster it goes.

I've learned…
That we should be glad God doesn't give us everything we ask for.

I've learned…
That money doesn't buy class.

I've learned…
That it's those small daily happenings that make life so spectacular.

99

Entertaining!
Amazing!

I've learned...
That under everyone's hard shell is someone who wants to be appreciated and loved.

I've learned...
That the Lord didn't do it all in one day. What makes me think I can?

I've learned...
That to ignore the facts does not change the facts.

I've learned...
That when you plan to get even with someone, you are only letting that person continue to hurt you.

I've learned...
That love, not time, heals all wounds.

I've learned...
That the easiest way for me to grow as a person is to surround myself with people smarter than I am.

I've learned...
That everyone you meet deserves to be greeted with a smile.

I've learned...
That there's nothing sweeter than sleeping with your babies and feeling their breath on your cheeks.

I've learned...
That life is tough, but I'm tougher.

Exciting!
Emotional!

I've learned…
That opportunities are never lost, someone will take the ones you miss.

I've learned…
That when you harbor bitterness, happiness will dock elsewhere.

I've learned…
That I wish I could have told my Dad that I love him one more time before he passed away.

I've learned…
That one should keep his words both soft and tender, because tomorrow he may have to eat them.

I've learned…
That a smile is an inexpensive way to improve your looks.

I've learned…
That I can't choose how I feel, but I can choose what I do about it.

I've learned…
That when your newly born child holds your little finger in his little fist, that you're hooked for life.

I've learned…
That everyone wants to live on top of the mountain but all the happiness and growth occurs while you're climbing it.

Entertaining!
Amazing!

I've learned…
That it is best to give advice in only two circumstances: when it is requested and when it is a life threatening situation.

I've learned…
That the less time I have to work with, the more things I get done.

To all of you…Make sure you read all the way down to the last sentence.

✷✷✷

May there always be work for your hands to do;
May your purse always hold a coin or two;
May the sun always shine on your windowpane;
May a rainbow be certain to follow each rain;
May the hand of a friend always be near you;
May God fill your heart with gladness to cheer you.

✷✷✷

Subject: I'm glad you're in my dash!!!

I read of a man who stood to speak
At the funeral of a friend
He referred to the dates on her tombstone
From the beginning…to the end.

He noted that first came her date of birth
And spoke the following date with tears,
But he said what mattered most of all
Was the dash between those years.

102

(1934–1998)

For that dash represents all the time
That she spent alive on earth…
And now only those who loved her
Know what that little line is worth.

For it matters not, how much we own;
The cars…the house…the cash,
What matters is how we live and love
And how we spend our dash.

So think about this long and hard…
Are there things you'd like to change?
For you never know how much time is left,
That can still be rearranged.

If we could just slow down enough
To consider what's true and real,
And always try to understand
The way other people feel.

And be less quick to anger,
And show appreciation more
And love the people in our lives
Like we've never loved before.

If we treat each other with respect,
And more often wear a smile…

Entertaining!
Amazing!

World's Funniest and Greatest E-mails

Remembering that this special dash
May last only a little while.

So, when your eulogy's being read
With your life's actions to rehash…
Would you be proud of the things they say
About how you spent your dash?

❋ ❋ ❋

The first day of school our professor introduced himself and challenged us to get to know someone we didn't already know. I stood up to look around when a gentle hand touched my shoulder. I turned around to find a wrinkled, little old lady beaming up at me with a smile that lit up her entire being.

She said, "Hi, Handsome. My name is Rose. I'm eighty- seven years old. Can I give you a hug?"

I laughed and enthusiastically responded, "Of course you may!" and she gave me a giant squeeze.

"Why are you in college at such a young, innocent age?" I asked.

She jokingly replied, "I'm here to meet a rich husband, get married, have a couple of kids…"

"No, seriously," I asked. I was curious what may have motivated her to be taking on this challenge at her age.

"I always dreamed of having a college education and now I'm getting one!" she told me.

After class we walked to the student union building and shared a chocolate milkshake.

104

Exciting!
Emotional!

We became instant friends. Every day for the next three months we would leave class together and talk nonstop.

I was always mesmerized listening to this "time machine" as she shared her wisdom and experience with me. Over the course of the year, Rose became a campus icon and she easily made friends wherever she went. She loved to dress up and she revelled in the attention bestowed upon her from the other students. She was living it up.

At the end of the semester we invited Rose to speak at our football banquet. I'll never forget what she taught us. She was introduced and stepped up to the podium. As she began to deliver her prepared speech, she dropped her three by five cards on the floor. Frustrated and a little embarrassed she leaned into the microphone and simply said, "I'm sorry I'm so jittery. I gave up beer for Lent and this whiskey is killing me! I'll never get my speech back in order so let me just tell you what I know."

As we laughed she cleared her throat and began, "We do not stop playing because we are old; we grow old because we stop playing. There are only four secrets to staying young, being happy and achieving success:

You have to laugh and find humor every day. You've got to have a dream. When you lose your dreams, you die. We have so many people walking around who are dead and don't even know it! There is a huge difference between growing older and growing up. If you are nineteen years old and lie in bed for one full year and don't do one productive thing, you will turn twenty years old. If I am eighty-seven years old and stay in bed for a year and never do anything I will turn eighty-eight. Anybody can grow older. That doesn't take any talent or ability. The idea is to grow up by always finding the opportunity in change. Have no regrets.

105

Entertaining!
Amazing!

The elderly usually don't have regrets for what we did, but rather for things we did not do. The only people who fear death are those with regrets."

She concluded her speech by courageously singing "The Rose." She challenged each of us to study the lyrics and live them out in our daily lives.

At the year's end Rose finished the college degree she had begun all those years ago.

One week after graduation Rose died peacefully in her sleep. Over two thousand college students attended her funeral in tribute to the wonderful woman who taught by example that it's never too late to be all you can possibly be. When you finish reading this, please send this peaceful word of advice to your friends and family, they'll really enjoy it! These words have been passed along in loving memory of ROSE.

REMEMBER, GROWING OLDER IS MANDATORY. GROWING UP IS OPTIONAL.

We make a Living by what we get. We make a Life by what we give.

God promises a safe landing, not a calm passage. If God brings you to it, He will bring you through it.

※※※

At an airport I overheard a father and daughter in their last moments together. They had announced her plane's departure and standing near the door, he said to his daughter, "I love you, I wish you enough." She said, "Daddy, our life together has been more than enough. Your love is all I ever needed. I wish you enough, too, Daddy." They kissed good-bye and she left.

He walked over toward the window where I was seated. Standing there I could see he wanted and needed to cry. I tried not to intrude on his privacy, but he

welcomed me in by asking, "Did you ever say good-bye to someone knowing it would be forever?" "Yes, I have," I replied. Saying that brought back memories I had of expressing my love and appreciation for all my Dad had done for me. Recognizing that his days were limited, I took the time to tell him face to face how much he meant to me. So I knew what this man was experiencing. "Forgive me for asking, but why is this a forever good-bye?" I asked.

"I am old and she lives much too far away. I have challenges ahead and the reality is, her next trip back will be for my funeral," he said.

"When you were saying good-bye I heard you say, 'I wish you enough.' May I ask what that means?" He began to smile. "That's a wish that has been handed down from other generations. My parents used to say it to everyone." He paused for a moment and looking up as if trying to remember it in detail, he smiled even more.

"When we said 'I wish you enough,' we were wanting the other person to have a life filled with enough good things to sustain them," he continued and then turning toward me he shared the following as if he were reciting it from memory.

"I wish you enough sun to keep your attitude bright. I wish you enough rain to appreciate the sun more. I wish you enough happiness to keep your spirit alive. I wish you enough pain so that the smallest joys in life appear much bigger. I wish you enough gain to satisfy your wanting. I wish you enough loss to appreciate all that you possess. I wish enough "Hello's" to get you through the final "Good-bye." He then began to sob and walked away.

My friends and loved ones, I wish you ENOUGH!!! They say, "It takes a minute to find a special person, an hour to appreciate them, a day to love them, but then an entire life to forget them."

☀☀☀

107

Entertaining!
Amazing!

Five lessons to make you think about the way we treat people.

1 – First Important Lesson – Cleaning Lady

During my second month of college, our professor gave us a pop quiz. I was a conscientious student and had breezed through the questions, until I read the last one: "What is the first name of the woman who cleans the school?"

Surely this was some kind of joke. I had seen the cleaning woman several times. She was tall, dark-haired and in her 50s, but how would I know her name?

I handed in my paper, leaving the last question blank. Just before class ended, one student asked if the last question would count toward our quiz grade. "Absolutely," said the professor. "In your careers, you will meet many people. All are significant. They deserve your attention and care, even if all you do is smile and say 'hello'.

I've never forgotten that lesson. I also learned her name was Dorothy.

2. – Second Important Lesson – Pickup in the Rain

One night, at 11.30 p.m., an older African American woman was standing on the side of an Alabama highway trying to endure a lashing rainstorm. Her car had broken down and she desperately needed a ride. Soaking wet, she decided to flag down the next car.

A young white man stopped to help her, generally unheard of in those conflict-filled 1960s. The man took her to safety, helped her get assistance and put her into a taxicab. She seemed to be in a big hurry, but wrote down his address and thanked him.

Seven days went by and a knock came on the man's door. To his surprise, a giant console color TV was delivered to his home.

A special note was attached. It read "Thank you so much for assisting me on the highway the other night. The rain drenched not only my clothes, but also my

108

spirits. Then you came along. Because of you, I was able to make it to my dying husband's bedside just before he passed away. God bless you for helping me and unselfishly serving others."

Sincerely, Mrs. Nat King Cole.

3 – Third Important Lesson – Always remember those who serve.

In the days when an ice cream sundae cost much less, a 10-year-old boy entered a hotel coffee shop and sat at a table. A waitress put a glass of water in front of him. "How much is an ice cream sundae?" he asked. "Fifty cents," replied the waitress. The little boy pulled his hand out of his pocket and studied the coins in it. "Well how much is a plain dish of ice cream?" he inquired. By now more people were waiting for a table and the waitress was growing impatient. "Thirty-five cents," she brusquely replied.

The little boy again counted his coins. "I'll have the plain ice cream," he said. The waitress brought the ice cream, put the bill on the table and walked away. The boy finished the ice cream, paid the cashier and left.

When the waitress came back, she began to cry as she wiped down the table.

There, placed neatly beside the empty dish, were two nickels and five pennies. You see, he couldn't have the sundae, because he had to have enough left to leave her a tip.

4 – Fourth Important Lesson – The obstacle in Our Path

In ancient times, a King had a boulder placed on a roadway. Then he hid himself and watched to see if anyone would remove the huge rock.

Some of the king's wealthiest merchants and courtiers came by and simply walked around it. Many loudly blamed the King for not keeping the roads clear, but none did anything about getting the stone out of the way.

109

Entertaining!
Amazing!

Then a peasant came along carrying a load of vegetables. Upon approaching the boulder, the peasant laid down his burden and tried to move the stone to the side of the road. After much pushing and straining, he finally succeeded. After the peasant picked up his load of vegetables, he noticed a purse lying in the road where the boulder had been.

The purse contained many gold coins and a note from the King indicating that the gold was for the person who removed the boulder from the roadway. The peasant learned what many of us never understand! Every obstacle presents an opportunity to improve our condition.

5 – Fifth Important Lesson – Giving When it Counts.

Many years ago, when I worked as a volunteer at a hospital, I got to know a little girl named Liz who was suffering from a rare and serious disease. Her only chance of recovery appeared to be a blood transfusion from her 5-year-old brother, who had miraculously survived the same disease and had developed the antibodies needed to combat the illness. The doctor explained the situation to her little brother, and asked the little boy if he would be willing to give his blood to his sister. I saw him hesitate for only a moment before taking a deep breath and saying, "Yes, I'll do it if it will save her."

As the transfusion progressed, he lay in bed next to his sister and smiled, as we all did, seeing the color returning to her cheek. Then his face grew pale and his smile faded. He looked up at the doctor and asked with a trembling voice, "Will I start to die right away?" Being young the little boy had misunderstood the doctor; he thought he was going to have to give his sister all of his blood in order to save her.

Now you have 2 choices.

Exciting!
Emotional!

1. Delete this email, or

2. Forward it to people you care about and might get a little lift from reading it…as I did. I hope that you will choose No. 2 and remember. "Work like you don't need the money, love like you've never been hurt, and dance like you do when nobody's watching."

NOW more than ever – Peace…Pass It On…Pay It Forward.

✹✹✹

I'll be happy when…We convince ourselves that life will be better after we get married, have a baby, then another. Then we are frustrated that the kids aren't old enough and we'll be more content when they are. After that, we're frustrated that we have teenagers to deal with. We will certainly be happy when they are out of that stage. We tell ourselves that our life will be complete when our spouse gets his or her act together, when we get a nicer car, when we are able to go on a nice vacation or when we retire. The truth is there's no better time to be happy than right now. If not now, when? Your life will always be filled with challenges. It's best to admit this to yourself and decide to be happy anyway. Happiness is the way. So, treasure every moment that you have and treasure it more because you shared it with someone special, special enough to spend your time with and remember that time waits for no one. So, stop waiting.

✹✹✹

Entertaining!
Amazing!

How To Stay Young
(George Carlin)

1. Throw out nonessential numbers. This includes age, weight and height. Let the doctor worry about them. That is why you pay him/her.
2. Keep only cheerful friends. The grouches pull you down.
3. Keep learning. Learn more about the computer, crafts, gardening, whatever. Never let the brain idle. "An idle mind is the devil's workshop." And the devil's name is Alzheimer's.
4. Enjoy the simple things.
5. Laugh often, long and loud. Laugh until you gasp for breath.
6. The tears happen. Endure, grieve, and move on. The only person who is with us our entire life, is ourselves. Be ALIVE while you are alive.
7. Surround yourself with what you love, whether it's family, pets, keepsakes, music, plants, hobbies, whatever. Your home is your refuge.
8. Cherish your health. If it is good, preserve it. If it is unstable, improve it. If it is beyond what you can improve, get help.
9. Don't take guilt trips. Take a trip to the mall, to the next county, to a foreign country, but NOT to where the guilt is.
10. Tell the people you love that you love them at every opportunity.

AND ALWAYS REMEMBER:

Life is not measured by the number of breaths we take, but by the moments that take our breath away. If you don't send this to at least eight people…who cares?

❈ ❈ ❈

112

Exciting!
Emotional!

Today…I wish you a day of ordinary miracles.
A fresh cup of coffee you didn't have to make yourself,
An unexpected phone call from an old friend,
I wish you a day of little things to rejoice in:
The fastest line at the grocery store,
A good sing along song on the radio,
Your keys right where you look.
I wish you a day of happiness and perfection, little bite-size pieces of perfection.
I wish you a day of peace, happiness and joy.

☀☀☀

My mother taught me…TO APPRECIATE A JOB WELL DONE.
"If you're going to kill each other, do it outside – I just finished cleaning"

My mother taught me…about RELIGION
"You'd better pray that will come out of the carpet"

My mother taught me…about TIME TRAVEL
"If you don't behave, I'm going to knock you into the middle of next week"

My mother taught me…about LOGIC
"Because I said so, that's why"

My mother taught me…about FORESIGHT
"Make sure you wear clean underwear, in case you're in an accident"

My mother taught me…about IRONY
"Keep laughing and I'll give you something to cry about"

Entertaining!
Amazing!

My mother taught me…about the science of OSMOSIS
"Shut your mouth and eat your supper"

My mother taught me…about CONTORTIONISM
"Will you look at the dirt on the back of your neck!"

My mother taught me…about STAMINA
"You'll sit there 'til all that spinach is finished!"

My mother taught me…about WEATHER
"It looks as if a tornado swept through your room."

My mother taught me…about HYPOCRISY
"If I've told you once, I've told you a million times—don't exaggerate!!!"

My mother taught me…about BEHAVIOR MODIFICATION
"Stop acting like your father!"

My mother taught me…about ENVY
"There are millions of less fortunate children in the world who don't have wonderful parents like you do!"

✹✹✹

Friends ~~~ Best Friends

Friend: calls your parents by Mr. and Mrs.
Best friend: calls your parents Mom and Dad.

Friend: has never seen you cry.
Best friend: has always had the best shoulder to cry on.

114

*Exciting!
Emotional!*

Friend: never asks for anything to eat or drink.
Best friend: opens the fridge and makes herself/himself at home.

Friend: asks you to write down your number.
Best friend: they ask you for their number (cuz he/she can't remember it).

Friend: borrows your stuff for a few days then gives it back.
Best friend: has a closet full of your stuff.

Friend: only knows a few things about you.
Best friend: could write a biography on your life story.

Friend: will leave you behind if that is what the crowd is doing.
Best friend: will always go with you.

❋❋❋

    I. Thou shalt not be perfect, or even try to be.
   II. Thou shalt not try to be all things to all people.
  III. Thou shalt sometimes leave things undone.
  IV. Thou shalt not spread thyself too thin.
   V. Thou shalt learn to say "no".
  VI. Thou shalt schedule time for thyself and for thy support network.
 VII. Thou shalt switch thyself off, and do nothing regularly.
VIII. Thou shalt not even feel guilty for doing nothing, or saying no.
  IX. Thou shalt be boring, untidy, inelegant, and unattractive at times.
   X. Especially, thou shalt not be thine own worst enemy. Be thine own best friend.

Entertaining!
Amazing!

※ ※ ※

Subject: The Donkey

One day a farmer's donkey fell down into a well. The animal cried piteously for hours as the farmer tried to figure out what to do.

Finally he decided the animal was old, and the well needed to be covered up anyway; it just wasn't worth it to retrieve the donkey. He invited all his neighbors to come over and help him. They all grabbed a shovel and began to shovel dirt into the well.

At first, the donkey realized what was happening and cried horribly. Then, to everyone's amazement, he quieted down. A few shovel loads later, the farmer finally looked down the well, and was astonished at what he saw. With every shovel of dirt that hit his back, the donkey was doing something amazing. He would shake it off and take a step up. As the farmer's neighbors continued to shovel dirt on top of the animal, he would shake it off and take a step up. Pretty soon, everyone was amazed as the donkey stepped up over the edge of the well and trotted off!

Life is going to shovel dirt on you, all kinds of dirt. The trick to getting out of the well is to shake it off and take a step up. Each of our troubles is a stepping stone. We can get out of the deepest wells just by not stopping, never giving up! Shake it off and take a step up!

Remember these five simple rules to be happy:

1. Free your heart from hatred.
2. Free your mind from worries.
3. Live simply.
4. Give more.
5. Expect less.

116

Exciting!
Emotional!

Now, enough of that crap.

The donkey later came back and kicked the shit out of the farmer who tried to bury him. Moral: When you try to cover your ass, it always comes back to get you.

✺ ✺ ✺

Slow Dance

Have you ever watched kids
On a merry-go-round?

Or listened to the rain
Slapping on the ground?

Ever followed a butterfly's erratic flight?
Or gazed at the sun into the fading night?

You better slow down.
Don't dance so fast.

Time is short.
The music won't last.

Do you run through each day
On the fly?

When you ask "How are you?"
Do you hear the reply?

When the day is done
Do you lie in your bed

117

With the next hundred chores
Running through your head?

You'd better slow down
Don't dance so fast.

Time is short.
The music won't last.

Ever told your child,
We'll do it tomorrow?

And in your haste,
Not see his sorrow?

Ever lost touch,
Let a good friendship die

Cause you never had time
To call and say, "hi"

You'd better slow down.
Don't dance so fast.

Time is short.
The music won't last.

When you run so fast to get somewhere
You miss half the fun of getting there.

Exciting!
Emotional!

When you worry and hurry through your day,
It is like an unopened gift...

Thrown away.
Life is not a race.

Do take it slower
Hear the music

Before the song is over.

☀☀☀

For the garden of your daily living, plant three rows of peas:

    1. Peace of mind
    2. Peace of heart
    3. Peace of soul

Plant four rows of squash:

    1. Squash gossip
    2. Squash indifference
    3. Squash grumbling
    4. Squash selfishness

Plant four rows of lettuce:

    1. Lettuce be faithful
    2. Lettuce be kind
    3. Lettuce be patient
    4. Lettuce really love one another.

Entertaining!
Amazing!

World's Funniest and Greatest E-mails

No garden is without turnips:
1. Turnip for meetings
2. Turnip for service
3. Turnip to help one another

To conclude our garden we must have thyme:
1. Thyme for each other
2. Thyme for family
3. Thyme for friends

Water freely with patience and cultivate with love. There is much fruit in your garden because you reap what you sow.

✸✸✸

LIFE IS SHORT, DANCE NAKED and WIGGLE YOUR BUTT!

✸✸✸

A Friend…
(A)ccepts you as you are
(B)elieves in "you"
(C)alls you just to say "HI"
(D)oesn't give up on you
(E)nvisions the whole of you (even the unfinished parts)
(F)orgives your mistakes
(G)ives unconditionally
(H)elps you
(I)nvites you over

(J)ust "be" with you
(K)eeps you close at heart
(L)oves you for who you are
(M)akes a difference in your life
(N)ever Judges
(O)ffers support
(P)icks you up
(Q)uiets your fears
(R)aises your spirits
(S)ays nice things about you
(T)ells you the truth when you need to hear it
(U)nderstands you
(V)alues you
(W)alks beside you
(X)-plains thing you don't understand
(Y)ells when you won't listen and
(Z)aps you back to reality

✺ ✺ ✺

Time Gets Better With Age

I learned that I like my teacher because she cries when we sing "Silent Night".
Age 5

I learned that our dog doesn't want to eat my broccoli either.
Age 7

121

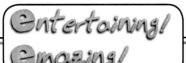

I learned that when I wave to people in the country, they stop what they are doing and wave back.
Age 9

I learned that just when I get my room the way I like it, Mom makes me clean it up again.
Age 12

I learned that if you want to cheer yourself up, you should try cheering someone else up.
Age 14

I learned that although it's hard to admit it, I'm secretly glad my parents are strict with me.
Age 15

I learned that silent company is often more healing than words of advice.
Age 24

I learned that brushing my child's hair is one of life's great pleasures.
Age 26

I learned that wherever I go, the world's worst drivers have followed me there.
Age 29

I learned that if someone says something unkind about me, I must live so that no one will believe it.
Age 30

I learned that there are people who love you dearly but just don't know how to show it.
Age 42

I learned that you can make some one's day by simply sending them a little note.
Age 44

I learned that the greater a person's sense of guilt, the greater his or her need to cast blame on others.
Age 46

I learned that children and grandparents are natural allies.
Age 47

I learned that no matter what happens, or how bad it seems today, life does go on, and it will be better tomorrow.
Age 48

I learned that singing "Amazing Grace" can lift my spirits for hours.
Age 49

I learned that motel mattresses are better on the side away from the phone.
Age 50

I learned that you can tell a lot about a man by the way he handles these three things: a rainy day, lost luggage, and tangled Christmas tree lights.
Age 51

I learned that keeping a vegetable garden is worth a medicine cabinet full of pills.
Age 52

Entertaining!
Amazing!

World's Funniest and Greatest E-mails

I learned that regardless of your relationship with your parents, you miss them terribly after they die.
Age 53

I learned that making a living is not the same thing as making a life.
Age 58

I learned that if you want to do something positive for your children, work to improve your marriage.
Age 61

I learned that life sometimes gives you a second chance.
Age 62

I learned that you shouldn't go through life with a catchers mitt on both hands. You need to be able to throw something back.
Age 64

I learned that if you pursue happiness, it will elude you. But if you focus on your family, the needs of others, your work, meeting new people, and doing the very best you can, happiness will find you.
Age 65

I learned that whenever I decide something with kindness, I usually make the right decision.
Age 66

I learned that everyone can use a prayer.
Age 72

124

I learned that even when I have pains, I don't have to be one.
Age 82

I learned that every day you should reach out and touch someone. People love that human touch—holding hands, a warm hug, or just a friendly pat on the back.
Age 90

I learned that I still have a lot to learn.
Age 92

World's Funniest and Greatest E-mails

Chapter 4

Drunken, Elder, Kids Humor

Entertaining!
Amazing!

World's Funniest and Greatest E-mails

Gotta Love Drunk People!

A man and his wife are awakened at 3:00 in the morning by a loud pounding on the door.

The man gets up and goes to the door where a drunken stranger, standing in the pouring rain, is asking for a push.

"Not a chance," says the husband, "it is 3:00 in the morning!"

He slams the door and returns to bed.

"Who was that?" asked his wife.

"Just some drunk guy asking for a push," he answers.

"Did you help him?" she asks.

"No, I did not, it is 3:00 in the morning and it is pouring out there!"

"Well, you have a short memory," says his wife.

"Can't you remember about three months ago when we broke down and those two guys helped us? I think you should help him, and you should be ashamed of yourself."

The man does as he is told, gets dressed, and goes out into the pounding rain.

He calls out into the dark, "Hello, are you still there?"

"Yes" comes back the answer.

"Do you still need a push?" calls out the husband.

"Yes, please!" comes the reply from the dark.

"Where are you?" asks the husband.

"Over here on the swing!" replies the drunk.

☀☀☀

The other night I was invited out for a night with "the girls." I told my husband that I would be home by midnight, "I promise!"

Exciting!
Emotional!

Well, the hours passed and the champagne was going down way too easy.

Around 3:00 a.m., drunk as a skunk, I headed for home. Just as I got in the door, the cuckoo clock in the hall started up and cuckooed three times.

Quickly, realizing he'd probably wake up, I cuckooed another nine times. I was really proud of myself for coming up with such a quick-witted solution (even when smashed), in order to escape a possible conflict with him.

The next morning my husband asked me what time I got in, and I told him 12:00. He didn't seem disturbed at all. Whew! Got away with that one!

Then he said, "We need a new cuckoo clock."

When I asked him why, he said, "Well, last night our clock cuckooed three times, then said, "oh shit," cuckooed four more times, cleared its throat, cuckooed another three times, giggled, cuckooed twice more, and then tripped over the cat and farted."

❊❊❊

Two women go out one weekend without their husbands. As they came back, right before dawn, both of them drunk, they felt the urge to pee. They noticed the only place to stop was a cemetery. Scared and drunk, they stopped and decided to go there anyway.

The first one did not have anything to clean herself with, so she took off her panties and used them to clean herself and discarded them.

The second not finding anything either, thought "I'm not getting rid of my panties…" so she used the ribbon of a flower wreath to clean herself.

The morning after, the two husbands were talking to each other on the phone, and one says to the other:

129

Entertaining!
Amazing!

"We have to be on the look-out, it seems that these two were up to no good last night, my wife came home without her panties...".

The other one responded: "You're lucky, mine came home with a card stuck to her ass that read, "We will never forget you".

✳ ✳ ✳

"Sometimes when I reflect back on all the beer I drink I feel shamed. Then I look into the glass and think about the workers in the brewery and all of their hopes and dreams. If I didn't drink this beer, they might be out of work and their dreams would be shattered. Then I say to myself, "It is better that I drink this beer and let their dreams come true than be selfish and worry about my liver."
—Jack Handy

"I feel sorry for people who don't drink. When they wake up in the morning, that's as good as they're going to feel all day."
—Frank Sinatra

"An intelligent man is sometimes forced to be drunk to spend time with his fools."
—Ernest Hemingway

"When I read about the evils of drinking, I gave up reading."
—Henny Youngman

"24 hours in a day, 24 beers in a case. Coincidence? I think not."
—Stephen Wright

Exciting!
Emotional!

"When we drink, we get drunk. When we get drunk, we fall asleep. When we fall asleep, we commit no sin. When we commit no sin, we go to heaven.
Sooooo, let's all get drunk and go to heaven!"
—Brian O'Rourke

"Beer is proof that God loves us and wants us to be happy."
—Benjamin Franklin

"Without question, the greatest invention in the history of mankind is beer. Oh, I grant you that the wheel was also a fine invention, but the wheel does not go nearly as well with pizza."
—Dave Barry

"Beer: Helping Ugly People Have Sex Since 3000 B.C.!!!"
—Unknown

Remember "I" before "E", except in Budweiser.

To some it's a six-pack, to me it's a Support Group. Salvation in a can!

And saving the best for last, as explained by Cliff Clavin, of Cheers.

One afternoon at Cheers, Cliff Clavin was explaining the Buffalo Theory to his buddy Norm. Here's how it went:

"Well ya see, Norm, it's like this…A herd of buffalo can only move as fast as the slowest buffalo. And when the herd is hunted, it is the slowest and weakest ones at the back that are killed first. This natural selection is good for the herd as a whole, because the general speed and health of the whole group keeps improving by the regular killing of the weakest members. In much the same way, the human brain can only operate as fast as the slowest brain cells. Excessive intake of alcohol,

131

as we know, kills brain cells. But naturally, it attacks the slowest and weakest brain cells first. In this way, regular consumption of beer eliminates the weaker brain cells, making the brain a faster and more efficient machine. That's why you always feel smarter after a few beers."

※ ※ ※

A southern Baptist minister was completing a temperance sermon. With great statement he said, "If I had all the beer in the world, I'd take it and pour it into the river."

With even greater emphasis he said, "And if I had all the wine in the world, I'd take it and pour it into the river."

And then finally, he said, "And if I had all the whiskey in the world, I'd take it and pour it into the river."

Sermon complete, he then sat down.

The song leader stood very cautiously and announced with a smile, "For our closing song, let us sing Hymn #365 – "Shall We Gather at the River"

※ ※ ※

An elderly couple is vacationing in the West. Sam always wanted a pair of authentic cowboy boots. Seeing some on sale one day, he buys them and wears them home, walking proudly. He walks into their hotel room and says to his wife, "Notice anything different, Helen?" Helen looks him over. "Nope." Ed says excitedly, "Come on, Helen, take a good look."

"Notice anything different about me?"

Helen looks again. "Nope."

Exciting!
Emotional!

Frustrated, Ed storms off into the bathroom, undresses, and walks back into the room completely naked except for his boots.

Again he asks, a little louder this time, "Notice anything DIFFERENT?"

Helen looks up and says, "Ed, what's different? It's hanging down today, it was hanging down yesterday, it'll be hanging down again tomorrow."

Furious, Ed yells, "AND DO YOU KNOW WHY ITS HANGING DOWN, HELEN? IT'S HANGING DOWN BECAUSE IT'S LOOKING AT MY NEW BOOTS!"

To which Helen replies, "Shoulda bought a hat Ed. Shoulda bought a hat."

☀☀☀

An old woman is riding in an elevator in a very lavish New York City building, when a young and beautiful woman gets into the elevator, smelling of expensive perfume. She turns to the old woman and says arrogantly, "Romance by Ralph Lauren, $150 an ounce!"

Then another young and beautiful woman gets on the elevator, and also very arrogantly turns to the old woman saying, "Channel No. 5, $200 an ounce."

About three floors later, the old woman has reached her destination and is about to get off the elevator. Before she leaves, she looks both beautiful women in the eye, farts, then says…"Broccoli, 49 cents a pound."

☀☀☀

Entertaining!
Amazing!

Senior Sex

An elderly couple is enjoying an anniversary dinner together in a small tavern. The husband leans over and asks his wife, "Do you remember the first time we had sex together over fifty years ago? We went behind this tavern where you leaned against the fence and I made love to you."

"Yes," she says, "I remember it well."

"OK" he says, "How about taking a stroll 'round there again and we can do it for old time's sake."

"Ooooooh Henry, you devil, that sounds like a good idea," she answers.

There's a police officer sitting in the next booth listening to all this, and having a chuckle to himself. He thinks, "I've got to see these two old-timers having sex against a fence. I'll just keep an eye on them so there's no trouble."

So he follows them. They walk haltingly along, leaning on each other for support, aided by walking sticks. Finally they get to the back of the tavern and make their way to the fence.

The old lady lifts her skirt, takes her knickers down and the old man drops his trousers.

She turns around and as she hangs on to the fence, the old man moves in.

Instantly they erupt into the most furious sex that the policeman has ever seen. They are bucking and jumping like eighteen-year olds.

This goes on for about forty minutes! She's yelling, "Ohhh, God!"

He's hanging on to her lips for dear life. This is the most athletic sex imaginable. Finally they both collapse panting on the ground. The policeman is amazed. He thinks he has learned something about life that he didn't know.

After about half an hour of lying on the ground recovering, the old couple struggle to their feet and put their clothes back on.

Exciting!
Emotional!

The policeman, still watching, thinks, "That was truly amazing, he was going like a train. I've got to ask him what his secret is."

As the couple pass, he says to them, "That was something else. You must have been having sex for about forty minutes. How do you do it? You must have had a fantastic life together. Is there some sort of secret?"

"No, there's no secret," the old man says. "Fifty years ago that damn fence wasn't electric."

❋❋❋

Three sisters aged 92, 94 and 96 live in a house together. One night the 96-year old draws a bath. She puts her foot in and pauses. She yells to the other sisters, "Was I gettin' in or out of the bath?" The 94-year old yells back, "I don't know. I'll come up and see." She starts up the stairs and pauses. "Was I going up the stairs or down?" The 92-year old is sitting at the kitchen table having tea listening to her sisters. She shakes her head and says, "I sure hope I never get that forgetful." She knocks on wood for good measure. She then yells, "I'll come up and help both of you as soon as I see who's at the door."

❋❋❋

"How was your golf game, dear?" asked Jack's wife, Tracy.

"Well, I was hitting pretty well, but my eyesight's gotten so bad, I couldn't see where the ball went."

"You're seventy-five years old, Jack!" admonished his wife. "Why don't you take my brother Scott along?"

"But he's eighty-five and doesn't even play golf anymore," protested Jack.

Entertaining!
Amazing!

"Yes, but he's got perfect eyesight and can watch your ball for you," Tracy pointed out.

The next day Jack teed off with Scott looking on. Jack swung and the ball disappeared down the middle of the fairway. "Did you see where it went?" asked Jack.

"Yup," Scott answered.

"Well, where is it?" yelled Jack, peering off into the distance.

"I forgot."

☀☀☀

An old farmer had owned a large farm for several years. He had a large pond in the back forty, fixed up nice: picnic tables, horseshoe courts, basketball court, etc. The pond was properly shaped and fixed up for swimming when it was built.

One evening the old farmer decided to go down to the pond, as he hadn't been there for a while, and look it over. As he neared the pond, he heard voices shouting and laughing with glee. As he came closer he saw it was a bunch of young women skinny dipping in his pond.

He made the women aware of his presence and they all went to the deep end of the pond.

One of the women shouted to him, "We're not coming out until you leave!"

The old man replied, "I didn't come down here to watch you ladies swim or make you get out of the pond naked. I only came to feed the alligators."

Moral: Old age and treachery will triumph over youth and skill.

☀☀☀

136

Exciting!
Emotional!

An elderly gentleman who sat calmly in his pew without moving, seemed oblivious to the fact that God's ultimate enemy was in his presence.

So Satan walked up to the old man and said. "Don't you know who I am?"

The man replied, "Yep, sure do."

"Aren't you afraid of me?" Satan asked.

"Nope, sure ain't." said the man.

"Don't you realize I can kill you with a word?" asked Satan.

"Don't doubt it for a minute," returned the old man, in an even tone.

"Did you know that I could cause you profound, horrifying AGONY for All eternity?" persisted Satan.

"Yep," was the calm reply.

"And you're still not afraid?" asked Satan.

"Nope," said the old man.

More than a little perturbed, Satan asked, "Well, why aren't You afraid of me?"

The man calmly replied, "Been married to your sister for 48 years."

☀☀☀

Two old ladies were outside their retirement home having a smoke, when it started to rain. One of the ladies pulled out a condom, cut off the end, put it over her cigarette, and continued smoking.

Lady 1: What's that?

Lady 2: A condom. This way my cigarette doesn't get wet.

Lady 1: Where did you get it?

Lady 2: You can get them at any drugstore.

The next day, Lady 1 hobbles herself into the local drugstore and announces to the pharmacist that she wants a box of condoms.

Entertaining!
Amazing!

The guy, embarrassed, looks at her kind of strangely (she is, after all, over 80 years of age), but very delicately asks what brand she prefers.

Lady 1: "Doesn't matter son, as long as it fits a Camel." The pharmacist fainted.

✹✹✹

—Old Age

An old man goes into the Pharmacy and asks for viagra.

The pharmacists asked "How many?"

The man replied, "Just a few, maybe a half dozen. I cut each one into four pieces."

The pharmacist said, "That's too small a dose. That won't get you through sex."

The old fellow said, "Oh, I'm past eighty years old and I don't even think about sex anymore. I just want it to stick out far enough so I don't pee on my shoes.

✹✹✹

Sunday Morning Sex

Upon hearing that her elderly grandfather had just passed away, Katie went straight to her grandparent's house to visit her 95-year-old grandmother and comfort her. When she asked how her grandfather had died, her grandmother replied, "He had a heart attack while we were making love on Sunday morning.

Horrified, Katie told her grandmother that two people nearly 100 years old having sex would surely be asking for trouble.

"Oh no, my dear," replied granny. "Many years ago, realizing our advanced age, we figured out the best time to do it was when the church bells would start to

ring. It was just the right rhythm. Nice and slow and even. Nothing too strenuous, simply in on the Ding and out on the Dong."

She paused to wipe away a tear, and continued, "and if the damned ice cream truck hadn't come along, he'd still be alive today."

✳✳✳

Subject: Onery Grandmas

Three old ornery grandmas were sitting on a bench outside a nursing home.

About then an old man walked by, and one of the grandmas said, "We bet we can tell how old you are."

The old man said "there ain't no way you can guess it."

One of the ornery grandmas said: "Sure we can!

Drop your pants!"

He did.

The old grandmas stared at him for a while and then they all piped up and said, "You're 84 years old!"

The old man was stunned. "Amazing. How did you guess that?"

The ornery old grandmas, laughed and slapping their knees, said, "You told us yesterday."

✳✳✳

A dietician was once addressing a large audience in Chicago. "The material we put into our stomachs is enough to have killed most of us sitting here, years ago. Red meat is awful. Soft drinks erode your stomach lining.

Chinese food is loaded with MSG. Vegetables can be disastrous, and none of us realizes the long-term harm caused by the germs in our drinking water."

139

Entertaining!
Amazing!

"But there is one thing that is the most dangerous of all and we all have, or will, eat it. Can anyone here tell me what food it is that causes the most grief and suffering for years after eating it?"

A 75-year-old man in the front row stood up and said, "Wedding cake."

☀☀☀

Sitting on the side of the highway waiting to catch speeding drivers, a State Police Officer sees a car puttering along at 22 MPH. He thinks to himself, "This driver is just as dangerous as a speeder!" So he turns on his lights and pulls the driver over. Approaching the car, he notices that there are five old ladies—two in the front seat and three in the back wide-eyed and white as ghosts. The driver, obviously confused, says to him, "Officer, I don't understand, I was doing exactly the speed limit! What seems to be the problem?" "Ma'am," the officer replies, "you weren't speeding, but you should know that driving slower than the speed limit can also be a danger to other drivers." "Slower than the speed limit? No sir, I was doing the speed limit exactly…twenty-two miles an hour!" the old woman says a bit proudly. The State Police officer, trying to contain a chuckle explains to her that "22" was the route number, not the speed limit. A bit embarrassed, the woman grinned and thanked the officer for pointing out her error. "But before I let you go, Ma'am, I have to ask…Is everyone in this car OK? These women seem awfully shaken and they haven't muttered a single peep this whole time," the officer asks. "Oh, they'll be all right in a minute officer. We just got off Route 119."

☀☀☀

Ethel and Mabel, two elderly widows, were watching the folks go by from their park bench. Ethel said, "You know, Mabel, I've been reading this 'Sex and

*Exciting!
Emotional!*

Marriage' book and all they talk about is 'mutual orgasm'. 'Mutual orgasm' here and 'mutual orgasm' there – that's all they talk about. Tell me, Mabel, when your husband was alive, did you two ever have mutual orgasm?". Mabel thought for a long while. Finally, she shook her head and said, "No, I think we had State Farm."

Three old ladies were sitting side by side in their retirement home reminiscing. The first lady recalled shopping at the green grocers and demonstrated with her hands, the length and thickness of a cucumber she could buy for a penny. The second old lady nodded, adding that onions used to be much bigger and cheaper also, and demonstrated the size of two big onions she could buy for a penny a piece. The third old lady remarked, "I can't hear a word you're saying, but I remember the guy you're talking about."

❋❋❋

An elderly couple had been dating for some time. Finally they decided it might be time for marriage. But before tying the knot, they went out for a heart to heart talk over dinner about whether it would really work out.

They discussed finances, living arrangements, snoring, and so on. Finally, the gentleman decided it was time to broach the subject of their physical relationship. "How do you feel about sex?" he asked, rather trustingly.

"Well," she said, responding very carefully, "I'd have to say that I would like it infrequently."

The old gentleman sat quietly for a moment. Then looking over his glasses, he casually asked, "Was that one word or two?"

❋❋❋

Entertaining!
Amazing!

Subject: Why Parents Go Gray

The boss of a big company needed to call one of his employees about an urgent problem with one of the main computers, dialed the employee's home phone number and was greeted with a child's whisper, "Hello."

"Is your daddy home?" he asked.

"Yes," whispered the small voice.

"May I talk with him?"

The child whispered, "No."

Surprised, and wanting to talk with an adult, the boss asked, "Is your mommy there?"

"Yes,"

"May I talk with her?"

Again the small voice whispered, "No."

Hoping there was somebody with whom he could leave a message, the boss asked, "Is anybody else there?"

"Yes," whispered the child, "a policeman."

Wondering what a cop would be doing at his employee's home, the boss asked, "May I speak with the policeman?"

"No, he's busy," whispered the child.

"Busy doing what?"

"Talking to Daddy and Mommy and the Fireman," came the whispered answer.

Growing concerned and even worried as he heard what sounded like a helicopter through the earpiece on the phone the boss asked, "What is that noise?"

"A hello-copper" answered the whispering voice.

"What is going on there?" asked the boss, now alarmed.

142

Exciting/ Emotional/

In an awed whispering voice the child answered, "The search team just landed the hello-copper."

Alarmed, concerned, and even more than just a little frustrated the boss asked, "What are they searching for?"

Still whispering, the young voice replied along with a muffled giggle: "ME."

※※※

Daddy Long-Legs

A father watched his daughter playing in the garden. He smiled as he reflected on how sweet and innocent his little girl was. Just precious!

Suddenly she just stopped and stared at the ground. He went over to her and noticed she was looking at two spiders mating. "Daddy, what are those two spiders doing?" she asked. "They're mating," her father replied.

"What do you call the spider on top, Daddy?" she asked.

"That's a Daddy Longlegs." Her father answered.

"So, the other one is a Mommy Longlegs?" the little girl asked. "No," her father replied, "both of them are Daddy Longlegs."

The little girl thought for a moment, then took her foot and stomped them flat.

"Well, we're not having any of that shit in our garden."

※※※

Entertaining!
Amazing!

Not to far from the truth!

Attorney General Ashcroft is visiting an elementary school. After the typical civics presentation to the class, he announced, "Alright, boys and girls, you can all ask me questions now."

Young Bobby raises his hand and says, "I have three questions, sir:
1. How did Bush win the election with fewer votes than Gore?
2. Why are you using the USA Patriot Act to limit Americans' civil liberties?
3. Why hasn't the U.S. caught Osama Bin Laden yet?"

Just then the bell sounds and all the kids run out to the playground. Fifteen minutes later, the kids come back in class and Ashcroft says, "I'm sorry we were interrupted by the bell. Now, you can all ask me questions."

Young Charlene raises her hand and says, "I have five questions, sir:
1. How did Bush win the election with fewer votes than Gore?
2. Why are you using the USA Patriot Act to limit Americans' civil liberties?
3. Why hasn't the U.S. caught Osama Bin Laden yet?"
4. Why did the bell go off 20 minutes early?
5. Where's Bobby?"

❋❋❋

When I stopped the bus to pick up Chris for preschool, I noticed an older woman hugging him as he left the house.

"Is that your grandmother?" I asked.

"Yes, "Chris said. "She's come to visit us for Christmas."

"How nice," I said. "Where does she live?"

At the airport," Chris replied. "Whenever we want her, we just go out there and get her."

Exciting!
Emotional!

✳✳✳

I didn't know if my granddaughter had learned her colors yet, so I decided to test her. I would point out something and ask what color it was. She would tell me and always she was correct. But it was fun for me, so I continued. At last, she headed for the door, saying sagely, "Grandma, I think you should try to figure out some of these yourself!"

✳✳✳

When the mother returned from the grocery store, her small son pulled out the box of animal crackers he had begged for, then he spread the animal-shaped crackers all over the kitchen counter.

"What are you doing?" his Mom asked. "The box says you can't eat them if the seal is broken," the boy explained. "I'm looking for the seal."

✳✳✳

This little grandmother was surprised by her seven-year-old grandson one morning. He had made her coffee. She drank what was the worst cup of coffee in her life. When she got to the bottom, there were three of those little green army men in the cup.

She said, "Honey, what are these army men doing in my coffee?"

Her grandson said, "Grandma, it says on TV 'The best part of waking up is soldiers in your cup!'"

✳✳✳

In the supermarket a man was pushing a cart that contained a screaming, bellowing baby. The gentleman kept repeating softly, "Don't get excited, Albert; don't scream, Albert; don't yell, Albert; keep calm, Albert."

Entertaining!
Amazing!

A woman standing next to him said, "You certainly are to be commended for trying to soothe your son, Albert."

The man looked at her and said, "Lady, I'm Albert."

✷✷✷

A three-year-old boy went with his dad to see a new litter of kittens. On returning home, he breathlessly informed his mother, "There were two boy kittens and two girl kittens."

"How did you know that?" his mother asked.

"Daddy picked them up and looked underneath," he replied. "I think it's printed on the bottom."

✷✷✷

While working for an organization that delivers lunches to elderly shut-ins, I used to take my four-year-old daughter on my afternoon rounds. She was unfailingly intrigued by the various appliances of old age, particularly the canes, walkers and wheelchairs. One day I found her staring at a pair of false teeth soaking in a glass. As I braced myself for the inevitable barrage of questions, she merely turned and whispered, "The tooth fairy will never believe this!"

✷✷✷

A little girl was watching her parents dress for a party. When she saw her dad donning his tuxedo, she warned, "Daddy, you shouldn't wear that suit."

"And why not, darling?"

"You know that it always gives you a headache the next morning."

✷✷✷

Exciting!
Emotional!

Chapter 4. Drunken, Elder, Kids Humor

While walking along the sidewalk in front of his church, our minister heard the intoning of a prayer that nearly made his collar wilt. Apparently, his five-year-old son and his playmates had found a dead robin. Feeling that proper burial should be performed, they had secured a small box and cotton batting, then dug a hole and made ready for the disposal of the deceased. The minister's son was chosen to say the appropriate prayers and with sonorous dignity intoned his version of what he thought his father always said: "Glory be unto the Faaaather. And unto the Soonnn…and into the hole he gooooes."

❋❋❋

A little girl had just finished her first week of school. "I'm just wasting my time," she said to her mother. "I can't read, I can't write, and they won't let me talk!"

❋❋❋

This is a heart warming story about the bond formed between a little girl and some construction workers. This makes you want to believe in the goodness of people and believe there is hope for the human race. A young family moved into a house next door to a vacant lot. One day a construction crew turned up to start building a house on the empty lot. The young family's 6-year-old daughter naturally took an interest in all the activity going on next door and started talking with the workers. She hung around and eventually the construction crew, gems-in-the-rough, all of them, more or less adopted her as a kind of project mascot. They chatted with her, let her sit with them while they had coffee and lunch breaks, and gave her little jobs to do here and there to make her feel important. At the end of the first week they even presented her with a pay envelope containing a dollar.

147

Entertaining!
Amazing!

World's Funniest and Greatest E-mails

The little girl took this home to her mother who said all the appropriate words of admiration and suggested that they take the dollar pay she had received to the bank the next day to start a savings account.

When they got to the bank the teller was equally impressed with the story and asked the little girl how she had come by her very own pay check at such a young age. The little girl proudly replied, "I've been working with a crew building a house all week."

"My goodness gracious," said the teller, "and will you be working on the house again this week too?"

She replied "I will if those useless sons of bitches at the lumber yard ever bring us any drywall that's worth a shit."

※※※

A stranger was seated next to Little Johnny on the plane when the stranger turned to Little Johnny and said, "Let's talk. I've heard that flights will go quicker if you strike up a conversation with your fellow passenger."

Little Johnny, who had just opened his book, closed it slowly, and said to the stranger, "What would you like to discuss?" "Oh, I don't know," said the stranger. "How about nuclear power?"

"OK," said Little Johnny. "That could be an interesting topic. But let me ask you a question first.

"A horse, a cow, and a deer all eat grass. The same stuff. Yet a deer excretes little pellets, while a cow turns out a flat patty, and a horse produces clumps of dried grass. Why do you suppose that is?"

"Jeez," said the stranger. "I have no idea."

148

Exciting!
Emotional!

"Well, then," said Little Johnny, "How is it that you feel qualified to discuss nuclear power when you don't know shit."

✹✹✹

Why We Love Children

A kindergarten pupil told his teacher he'd found a cat.
She asked him if it was dead or alive.
"Dead," she was informed.
"How do you know?" she asked her pupil.
"Because I pissed in its ear and it didn't move," answered the child innocently.
"You did WHAT?!?" the teacher exclaimed in surprise.
"You know," explained the boy, "I leaned over and went 'Pssst!' and it didn't move."

✹✹✹

A small boy is sent to bed by his father.
Five minutes later…
"Da-ad…"
"What?
"I'm thirsty. Can you bring drink of water?"
"No. You had your chance. Lights out."

Five minutes later:
"Da-aaaad…"
"WHAT?"
"I'm THIRSTY. Can I have a drink of water??"
"I told you NO!" If you ask again, I'll have to spank you!!"

149

Entertaining!
Amazing!

Five minutes later…

"Daaaa-aaaad…"

"WHAT!"

"When you come in to spank me, can you bring a drink of water?"

An exasperated mother, whose son was always getting into mischief, finally asked him, "How do you expect to get into Heaven?"

The boy thought it over and said, "Well, I'll run in and out and in and out and keep slamming the door until St Peter says, 'For Heaven's sake, Dylan, come in or stay out'."

※ ※ ※

One summer evening during a violent thunderstorm a mother was tucking her son into bed. She was about to turn off the light when he asked with a tremor in his voice, "Mommy, will you sleep with me tonight?"

The mother smiled and gave him a reassuring hug.

"I can't dear," she said. "I have to sleep in Daddy's room."

A long silence was broken at last by his shaky little voice: "The big sissy."

※ ※ ※

It was that time, during the Sunday morning service, for the children's sermon. All the children were invited to come forward. One little girl was wearing a particularly pretty dress and, as she sat down, the pastor leaned over and said, "That is a very pretty dress. Is it your Easter Dress?"

The little girl replied, directly into the pastor's clip-on microphone, "Yes, and my Mom says it's a bitch to iron."

※ ※ ※

150

Chapter 4. Drunken. Elder. Kids Humor

When I was six months pregnant with my third child, my three-year old came into the room when I was just getting ready to get into the shower. She said, "Mommy, you are getting fat!"

I replied, "Yes, honey, remember Mommy has a baby growing in her tummy."

"I know," she replied, but what's growing in your butt?"

❋❋❋

A little boy was doing his math homework. He said to himself, "Two plus five, that son of a bitch is seven.

Three plus six, that son of a bitch is nine…"

His mother heard what he was saying and gasped, "What are you doing?"

The little boy answered, "I'm doing my math homework, Mom."

"And this is how your teacher taught you to do it?" the mother asked.

"Yes," he answered

Infuriated, the mother asked the teacher the next day, "What are you teaching my son in math?"

The teacher replied, "Right now, we are learning addition."

The mother asked, "And are you teaching them to say two plus two, that son of a bitch is four?"

After the teacher stopped laughing, she answered, "What I taught them was, two plus two, THE SUM OF WHICH, is four."

❋❋❋

One day the first grade teacher was reading the story of Chicken Little to her class. She came to the part of the story where Chicken Little tried to warn the farmer.

Entertaining!
Amazing!

She read, "…and so Chicken Little went up to the farmer and said, "The sky is falling, the sky is falling!"

The teacher paused then asked the class, "And what do you think that farmer said?"

One little girl raised her hand and said, "I think he said: 'Holy Shit! A talking chicken!'"

The teacher was unable to teach for the next 10 minutes.

※※※

A little boy was in a relative's wedding. As he was coming down the aisle he would take two steps, stop and turn to the crowd (alternating between bride's side and groom's side).

While facing the crowd, he would put his hands up like claws and roar. So it went, step, step, "ROAR," step, step, "ROAR," all the way down the aisle. As you can imagine, the crowd was near tears from laughing so hard by the time he reached the pulpit.

The little boy, however, was getting more and more distressed from all the laughing and was also near tears by the time he reached the pulpit.

When asked what he was doing, the child sniffed and said, "I was being the Ring Bear!"

※※※

Two young boys walked into a pharmacy one day, picked out a box of Tampax and proceeded to the check-out counter.

The man at the counter asked the older boy, "Son, how old are you?"

"Eight," the boy replied. The man continued, "Do you know how these are used?"

152

The boy replied, "Not exactly, but they aren't for me. They are for my brother, he's four. We saw on TV that if you use these you would be able to swim and ride a bike. He can't do either one, yet.

✻✻✻

It was late at night and Heidi, who was expecting her second child was home alone with her 3-year-old daughter Katelyn. When Heidi started going into labor, she called "911."

Due to a power outage at the time, only one paramedic responded to the call. The house was very, very dark, so the paramedic asked Katelyn to hold a flashlight high over her mommy so he could see while he helped deliver the baby.

Very diligently, Katelyn did as she was asked. Heidi pushed and pushed, and after a little while Connor was born.

The paramedic lifted him by his little feet and spanked him on his bottom. Connor began to cry.

The paramedic then thanked Katelyn for her help and asked the wide-eyed three-year old what she thought about what she had just witnessed.

Katelyn quickly responded, "He shouldn't have crawled in there in the first place. Smack him again!"

✻✻✻

A mother and father took their 6-year-old son to a nude beach. As the boy walked along the beach, he noticed that some of the ladies had boobs bigger than his mother's, and asked her why.

She told her son, "The bigger they are the dumber the person is."

153

Entertaining!
Amazing!

The boy, pleased with the answer, goes to play in the ocean but returns to tell his mother that many of the men have larger "units" than his dad.

His Mother replied, "The bigger they are the dumber the person is." Again satisfied with this answer, the boy returns to the ocean to play.

Shortly after, the boy returned again. He promptly told his mother, "Daddy is talking to the dumbest girl on the beach, and the longer he talks, the dumber he gets."

✻✻✻

A first-grade teacher, Ms. Brooks was having trouble with one of her students. The teacher asked, "Harry, what is your problem?"

Harry answered, "I'm too smart for the first-grade. My sister is in the third-grade and I'm smarter than she is! I think I should be in the third grade too!"

Ms. Brooks had had enough. She took Harry to the principal's office. While Harry waited in the outer office, the teacher explained to the principal what the situation was. The principal told Ms. Brooks he would give the boy a test and if he failed to answer any of his questions he was to go back to the first-grade and behave. She agreed.

Harry was brought in and the conditions were explained to him and he agreed to take the test.

Principal: "What is 3 × 3?" Harry: "9".

Principal: "What is 6 × 6?" Harry: "36".

And so it went with every question the principal thought a third-grade should know. The principal looks at Ms. Brooks and tells her, "I think Harry can go to the third-grade."

Ms. Brooks says to the principal, "Let me ask him some questions?"

The principal and Harry both agree.

Ms. Brooks asks, "What does a cow have four of that I have only two of?"

Harry, after a moment: "Legs."

Ms. Brooks: "What is in your pants that you have but I do not have?"

The principal wondered, why does she ask such a question!

Harry replied: "Pockets."

Ms. Brooks: "What does a dog do that a man steps into?"

Harry: "Pants"

Ms. Brooks: "What's starts with a C and ends with a T, is hairy, oval, and contains thin whitish liquid?"

Harry: "Coconut"

Ms. Brooks: "What goes in hard and pink then comes out soft and sticky"?

Harry: "Bubblegum"

Ms. Brooks: "What does a man do standing up, a woman do sitting down and a dog does on three legs?"

Harry: "Shake hands"

Ms. Brooks: Now I will ask some "Who am I" sort of questions, okay?

Harry: "Yep".

Ms. Brooks: "You stick your poles inside me. You tie me down to get me up. I get wet before you do."

Harry: "Tent"

Ms. Brooks: "A finger goes in me. You fiddle with me when you're bored. The best man always has me first."

The Principal was looking restless and bit tense.

Harry: "Wedding Ring"

Entertaining!
Amazing!

Ms. Brooks: "I come in many sizes. When I'm not well, I drip. When you blow me, you feel good".

Harry: "Nose".

Ms. Brooks: "I have a stiff shaft. My tip penetrates, I come with a quiver".

Harry: "Arrow"

Ms. Brooks: "What word starts with an 'F' and ends in 'K' that means a lot of heat and excitement?"

Harry: "Firetruck"

The principal breathed a sigh of relief and told the teacher, "Put Harry in the fifth-grade, I got the last ten questions wrong myself."

※ ※ ※

A little boy comes down to breakfast. Since he lives on a farm with his family, his mother asks if he had done his chores.

"Not yet." says the little boy.

His mother tells him he can't have any breakfast until he does his chores.

Well, he's a little pissed, so he goes to feed the chickens and kicks a chicken. He goes to feed the cows and kicks a cow. He goes to feed the pigs and kicks a pig.

He goes back in for breakfast and his mother gives him a bowl of dry cereal.

"How come I don't get any eggs and bacon? Why don't I have any milk in my cereal?" the kid asks.

"Well," his mother says, "I saw you kick a chicken, so you don't get any eggs for a week. I saw you kick the pig, so you don't get any bacon for a week, either. I also saw you kick the cow, so for a week you aren't getting any milk."

Just then, his father comes down for breakfast and kicks the cat as he's walking into the kitchen.

The little boy looks at his mother with a smile and says, "Are you going to tell! him or should I?"

※ ※ ※

Little David comes home from first grade and tells his father that they learned about the history of Valentine's Day.

"Since Valentine's day is for a Christian saint and we're Jewish," he asks, "will God get mad at me for giving someone a valentine?"

David's father thinks a bit, then says "No, I don't think God would get mad. Who do you want to give a valentine to?"

"Osama Bin Laden," David says.

"Why Osama Bin Laden," his father asks in shock.

"Well," David says, "I thought that if a little American Jewish boy could have enough love to give Osama a valentine, he might start to think that maybe we're not all bad, and maybe start loving people a little bit.

And if other kids saw what I did and sent valentines to Osama, he'd love everyone a lot.

And then he'd start going all over the place to tell everyone how much he loved them and how he didn't hate anyone anymore.

His father's heart swells and he looks at his boy with newfound pride.

"David, that's the most wonderful thing I've ever heard."

"I know," David says, "and once that gets him out in the open, the Marines could blow the shit out of him."

157

Entertaining! Amazing!

World's Funniest and Greatest E-mails

Exciting!
Emotional!

Chapter 5

Religion

159

This is so powerful…I do hope that you take the time to read it.

One day a while back, a man, his heart heavy with grief, was walking in the woods. As he thought about his life this day, he knew many things were not right. He thought about those who had lied about him back when he had a job. His thoughts turned to those who had stolen his things and cheated him. He remembered family that had passed on. His mind turned to the illness he had that no one could cure. His very soul was filled with anger, resentment and frustration.

Standing there this day, searching for answers he could not find, knowing all else had failed him, he knelt at the base of an old oak tree to seek the one he knew would always be there. And with tears in his eyes, he prayed: "Lord, you have done wonderful things for me in this life. You have told me to do many things for you, and I happily obeyed. Today, you have told me to forgive. I am sad, Lord, because I cannot. I don't know how. It is not fair Lord. I didn't deserve these wrongs that were done against me and I shouldn't have to forgive. As perfect as your way is Lord, this one thing I cannot do, for I don't know how to forgive. My anger is so deep Lord, I fear I may not hear you, but I pray that you teach me to do this one thing I cannot do – Teach me to forgive."

As he knelt there in the quiet shade of that old oak tree, he felt something fall onto his shoulder. He opened his eyes. Out of the corner of one eye, he saw something red on his shirt. He could not turn to see what it was because where the oak tree had been was a large square piece of wood in the ground. He raised his head and saw two feet held to the wood with a large spike through them. He raised his head more, and tears came to his eyes as he saw Jesus hanging on a cross. He saw spikes in His hands, a gash in His side, a torn and battered body, deep thorns sunk into His head. Finally he saw the suffering and pain on His precious face. As their eyes met, the man's tears turned to sobbing, and Jesus began to speak.

160

Exciting!
Emotional!

"Have you ever told a lie," he asked? The man answered, "yes, Lord."
"Have you ever been given too much change and kept it?"
The man answered, "yes, Lord." And the man sobbed more and more.
"Have you ever taken something from work that wasn't yours," Jesus asked?
And the man answered, "yes, Lord."
"Have you ever sworn, using my Father's name in vain?"
The man, crying now, answered, "yes, Lord."

As Jesus asked many more times, "have you ever?" The man's crying became uncontrollable, for he could only answer, "yes, Lord." Then Jesus turned His head from one side to the other, and the man felt something fall on his other shoulder. He looked and saw that it was the blood of Jesus.

When he looked back up, his eyes met those of Jesus, and there was a look of love the man had never seen or known before. Jesus said, "I didn't deserve this either, but I forgive you."

It may be hard to see how you're going to get through something, but when you look back in life, you realize how true this statement is. Read the first line slowly and let it sink in. This is simple, and important.

Read on…This first line is deep.

If God brings you to it – He will bring you through it. Lord I love You and I need You, come into my heart, today. For without You I can do nothing.

Pass this message to seven people except you and me. You will receive a miracle tomorrow. If you choose not, then you refuse to bless someone else. Don't ignore and God will bless you.

※ ※ ※

Entertaining!
Amazing!

A child asked God, "They tell me you are sending me to earth tomorrow, but how am I going to live there being so small and helpless?"

"Your angel will be waiting for you and will take care of you."

The child further inquired, "But tell me, here in heaven I don't have to do anything but sing and smile to be happy."

God said, "Your angel will sing for you and will also make you happy."

Again the child asked, "And how am I going to be able to understand when people talk to me if I don't know the language?"

God said, "Your angel will tell you the most beautiful and sweet words you will ever hear, and with much patience and care, your angel will teach you how to speak."

"And what am I going to do when I want to talk to you?"

God said, "Your angel will place your hands together and will teach you how to pray."

"Who will protect me?"

God said, "Your angel will defend you even if it means risking its life."

"But I will always be sad because I will not see you anymore."

God said, "Your angel will always talk to you about me and will teach you the way to come back to me, even though I will always be next to you."

At that moment there was much peace in heaven, but voices from Earth could be heard and the child hurriedly asked, "God, if I am to leave now, please tell me my angel's name."

"You will simply call her 'Mom'."

☀ ☀ ☀

162

Exciting!
Emotional!

The Shoes

My alarm went off
It was Sunday again.
I was sleepy and tired,
My one day to sleep in.

But the guilt I would feel
The rest of the day
Would have been too much,
So I'd go and I'd pray.

I showered and shaved,
I adjusted my tie,
I got there and sat
In a pew just in time.

Bowing my head in prayer
As I closed my eyes,
I saw the shoe of the man next to me
Touching my own. I sighed.

With plenty of room on either side,
I thought, "Why must our soles touch?"
It bothered me, his shoe touching mine,
But it didn't bother him much.

Entertaining!
Amazing!

A prayer began: "Our Father"
I thought, "This man with the shoes has no pride.
They're dusty, worn, and scratched
Even worse, there are holes on the side!"

"Thank You for blessings," the prayer went on.
The shoe man said a quiet "Amen."
I tried to focus on the prayer,
But my thoughts were on his shoes again.

Aren't we supposed to look our best
When walking through that door?
"Well, this certainly isn't it," I thought,
Glancing toward the floor.

Then the prayer had ended
And the songs of praise began.
The shoe man was certainly loud,
Sounding proud as he sang.

His voice lifted the rafters,
His hands were raised high,
The Lord could surely hear
The shoe man's voice from the sky.

It was time for the offering
And what I threw in was steep.
I watched as the shoe man reached
Into his pockets so deep.

Exciting!
Emotional!

I saw what was pulled out,
What the shoe man put in,
Then I heard a soft "clink"
As when silver hits tin.

The sermon really bored me
To tears, and that's no lie
It was the same for the shoe man,
For tears fell from his eyes.

At the end of the service,
As is the custom here,
We must greet new visitors
And show them all good cheer.

But I felt moved somehow
And wanted to meet shoe man
So after the closing prayer,
I reached over and shook his hand.

He was old and his skin was dark,
And his hair was truly a mess
But I thanked him for coming,
For being our guest.

He said, "My name's Charlie,
I'm glad to meet you, my friend."
There were tears in his eyes
But he had a large, wide grin.

165

Entertaining!
Amazing!

"Let me explain," he said
Wiping tears from his eyes.
"I've been coming here for months,
And you're the first to say 'Hi.'"

"I know that my appearance
Is not like all the rest,
But I really do try
To always look my best."

"I always clean and polish my shoes
Before my very long walk
But by the time I get here,
They're dirty and dusty, like chalk."

My heart filled with pain and
I swallowed to hide my tears
As he continued to apologize
For daring to sit so near.

He said, "When I get here,
I know I must look a sight.
But I thought if I could touch you,
Then maybe our souls might unite."

I was silent for a moment
Knowing whatever was said
Would pale in comparison.
I spoke from my heart, not my head.

166

Exciting!
Emotional!

"Oh, you've touched me," I said,
"and taught me, in part,
That the best of any man
Is what is found in his heart."

The rest, I thought,
This shoe man will never know...
Like just how thankful I really am
That his dirty old shoe touched my soul.

❋❋❋

A man and his dog were walking along a road. The man was enjoying the scenery, when it suddenly occurred to him that he was dead.

He remembered dying, and that the dog walking beside him had been dead for years. He wondered where the road was leading them.

After a while, they came to a high, white stone wall along one side of the road. It looked like fine marble. At the top of a long hill, it was broken by a tall arch that glowed in the sunlight. When he was standing before it, he saw a magnificent gate in the arch that looked like mother of pearl, and the street that led to the gate looked like pure gold.

He and the dog walked toward the gate, and as he got closer, he saw a man at a desk to one side. When he was close enough, he called out,

"Excuse me, where are we?"

"This is Heaven, sir," the man answered.

"Wow! Would you happen to have some water?" the man asked.

"Of course, sir. Come right in, and I'll have some ice water brought right up." The man gestured, and the gate began to open.

Entertaining!
Amazing!

"Can my friend," gesturing toward his dog, "come in, too?" the traveler asked.

"I'm sorry, sir, but we don't accept pets."

The man thought a moment and then turned back toward the road and continued the way he had been going with his dog.

After another long walk, and at the top of another long hill, he came to a dirt road which led through a farm gate that looked as if it had never been closed. There was no fence. As he approached the gate, he saw a man inside, leaning against a tree and reading a book.

"Excuse me!" he called to the reader. "Do you have any water?"

"Yeah, sure, there's a pump over there." The man pointed to a place that couldn't be seen from outside the gate. "Come on in."

"How about my friend here?" the traveler gestured to the dog.

"There should be a bowl by the pump." They went through the gate, and sure enough, there was an old fashioned hand pump with a bowl beside it. The traveler filled the bowl and took a long drink himself, then he gave some to the dog.

When they were full, he and the dog walked back toward the man who was standing by the tree waiting for them.

"What do you call this place?" the traveler asked.

"This is Heaven," was the answer.

"Well, that's confusing," the traveler said. "The man down the road said that was Heaven, too."

"Oh, you mean the place with the gold street and pearly gates? Nope. That's Hell."

"Doesn't it make you mad for them to use your name like that?"

"No. I can see how you might think so, but we're just happy that they screen out the folks who'll leave their best friends behind."

168

@xciting!
@motional!

Sometimes, we wonder why friends keep forwarding jokes to us without writing a word, maybe this could explain:

When you are very busy, but still want to keep in touch, guess what you do? You forward jokes.

When you have nothing to say, but still want to keep contact, you forward jokes.

When you have something to say, but don't know what, and don't know how, you forward jokes. And to let you know that you are still remembered, you are still important, you are still loved, you are still cared for, guess what you get? A forwarded joke.

So my friend, next time you get a joke, don't think that you've been sent just another forwarded joke, but that you've been thought of today and your friend on the other end of your computer wanted to send you a smile.

HAVE A GREAT DAY

☀☀☀

Everything I need to know about life, I learned from Noah's Ark...

One: Don't miss the boat.

Two: Remember that we are all in the same boat.

Three: Plan ahead. It wasn't raining when Noah built the Ark.

Four: Stay fit. When you're 600 years old, someone may ask you to do something really big.

Five: Don't listen to critics; just get on with the job that needs to be done.

Six: Build your future on high ground.

Seven: For safety's sake, travel in pairs.

Entertaining!
Amazing!

Eight: Speed isn't always an advantage. The snails were on board with the cheetahs.

Nine: When you're stressed, float a while.

Ten: Remember, the Ark was built by amateurs; the Titanic by professionals.

Eleven: No matter the storm, when you are with God, there's always a rainbow waiting.

NOW, wasn't that nice? Pass it along and make someone else smile, too.

☀☀☀

Priorities

I asked God to grant me patience.

God said, No. Patience is a byproduct of tribulations; it is not granted, it is earned.

I asked God to give me happiness.

God said, No. I give you blessings. Happiness is up to you.

I asked God to spare me pain.

God said, No. Suffering draws you apart from worldly cares and brings you closer to me.

I asked God to make my spirit grow.

God said, No. You must grow on your own, but I will prune you to make you fruitful.

I asked for all things that I might enjoy life.

God said, No. I will give you life so that you may enjoy all things.

exciting!
emotional!

Chapter 5. Religion

I ask God to help me LOVE others, as much as he loves me.
God said…Ahhhh, finally you have the idea.

If you love God, send this to ten people and back to the person that sent it.

Stop telling God how big your storm is.
Instead tell your storm how big your God is.

❋❋❋

Dear God,
Please put another holiday between Christmas and Easter. There is nothing good in there now. —Ginny

Dear God,
Thank you for the baby brother, but what I asked for was a puppy. I never asked for anything before. You can look it up. —Joyce

Dear Mr. God,
I wish you would not make it so easy for people to come apart. I had to have three stitches and a shot. —Janet

Dear God
If we come back as something, please don't let me be Jennifer Horton – because I hate her. —Denise

Dear God,
It rained for our whole vacation and is my father mad! He said some things about you that people are not supposed to say, but I hope you will not hurt him anyway. —Your friend (I am not going to tell you who I am).

Entertaining!
Amazing!

Dear God,
I read the Bible. What does begat mean? Nobody will tell me. —Love, Alison

Dear God,
How did you know you were God? —Charlene

Dear God,
Is it true my father won't get in Heaven if he uses his bowling words in the house? —Anita

Dear God,
I bet it's very hard for you to love all of everybody in the whole world. There are only four people in our family and I can never do it. —Ann

Dear God:
Did you really mean "Do Unto Others As They Do Unto You," because if you did then I'm going to fix my brother. —Darla

Dear God,
I like the story about Chanuka the best of all of them. You really made up some good ones. —Glenn

Dear God,
My Grandpa says you were around when he was a little boy. How far back do you go? —Love, Dennis

Dear God,
Who draws the lines around the countries? —Nan

172

Exciting!
Emotional!

Dear God,
It's o.k. that you made different religions but don't you get mixed up sometimes? —Arnold

Dear God,
Did you mean for a giraffe to look like that or was it an accident? —Norma

Dear God,
In Bible times did they really talk that fancy? —Jennifer

Dear God,
What does it mean you are a jealous God? I thought you had everything. —Jane

Dear God,
How come you did all those miracles in the old days and don't do any now? —Seymour

Dear God,
Please send Dennis Clark to a different camp this year. —Peter

Dear God,
Maybe Cain and Abel would not kill each other so much if they had their own rooms. It works with my brother. —Larry

Dear God,
I keep waiting for spring but it never did come yet. Don't forget. —Mark

Dear God,
You don't have to worry about me. I always look both ways. —Dean

Entertaining!
Amazing!

Dear God,
My brother told me about being born but it doesn't sound right. —Marsha

Dear God,
If you watch in Church on Sunday I will show you my new shoes. —Mickey D.

Dear God,
Is Reverend Coe a friend of yours, or do you just know him through business? —Donny

Dear God,
In Sunday School they told us what you do. Who does it when you are on vacation? —Jane

Dear God,
We read Thomas Edison made light. But in Sunday School they said you did it. So I bet he stole your idea. —Sincerely, Donna

Dear God,
I do not think anybody could be a better God. Well, I just want you to know but I am not just saying that because you are God. —Charles

Dear God,
It is great the way you always get the stars in the right places. —Jeff

Dear God,
I am doing the best I can. —Frank

174

Dear God,

I didn't think orange went with purple until I saw the sunset you made on Tuesday. That was cool. —Eugene

✸✸✸

THIS ONE IS FABULOUS!!! It was written by an 8-year old, Danny Dutton of Chula Vista, CA, for his third-grade homework assignment. The assignment was to explain God. Wonder if any of us could do as well?

Explain God

One of God's main jobs is making people. He makes them to replace the ones that die, so there will be enough people to take care of things on earth. He doesn't make grown-ups, just babies. I think because they are smaller and easier to make. That way He doesn't have to take up His valuable time teaching them to talk and walk. He can just leave that to mothers and fathers.

God's second most important job is listening to prayers. An awful lot of this goes on, since some people, like preachers and things, pray at times beside bed-time. God doesn't have time to listen to the radio or TV because of this. God sees everything and hears everything and is everywhere which keeps Him pretty busy. So you shouldn't go wasting His time by going over your Mom and Dad's head asking for something they said you couldn't have.

Atheists are people who don't believe in God. I don't think there are any in Chula Vista. At least there aren't any who come to our church.

Jesus is God's Son. He used to do all the hard work like walking on water and performing miracles and people finally got tired of Him preaching to them and they crucified Him. But He was good and kind, like His Father and He told His

175

Entertaining!
Amazing!

Father that they didn't know what they were doing and to forgive them and God said "O.K."

His Dad (God) appreciated everything that He had done and all His hard work on earth so He told Him He didn't have to go out on the road anymore. He could stay in heaven. So He did. And now He helps His Dad out by listening to prayers and seeing things which are important for God to take care of and which ones He can take care of Himself without having to bother God. Like a secretary, only more important. You can pray anytime you want and they are sure to help you because they got it worked out so one of them is on duty all the time.

You should always go to church on Sunday because it makes God happy, and if there's anybody you want to make happy, it's God. Don't skip church to do something you think will be more fun like going to the beach. This is wrong. And besides the sun doesn't come out at the beach until noon anyway.

If you don't believe in God, besides being an atheist, you will be very lonely, because your parents can't go everywhere with you, like to camp, but God can. It is good to know He's around you when you're scared in the dark or when you can't swim and you get thrown into real deep water by big kids. But…you shouldn't just always think of what God can do for you.

I figure God put me here and He can take me back anytime He pleases. And…that's why I believe in God.

Keep these thoughts with you throughout the coming years!
1. If God had a refrigerator, your picture would be on it.
2. If He had a wallet, your photo would be in it.
3. He sends you flowers every spring and a sunrise every morning.
4. Whenever you want to talk, He'll listen.

Exciting!
Emotional!

5. He could live anywhere in the universe, and He chose your heart.

6. What about the Christmas gift He sent you in Bethlehem—not to mention that Friday at Calvary.

Face it, He's crazy about you.

Send this to the people you're crazy about, I did as I thought this was pretty special, just like you.

Pass this on and brighten someone's day, and remember:
God answers Knee-Mail!

☀☀☀

God won't ask what your highest salary was, but He'll ask if you compromised your character to obtain it.

God won't ask how much overtime you worked, but He'll ask if your overtime work was for yourself or for your family.

God won't ask how many promotions you received, but He'll ask how you promoted others.

God won't ask what your job title was, but He'll ask if you performed your job to the best of your ability.

God won't ask what kind of car you drove, but He'll ask how many people you drove who didn't have transportation.

177

Entertaining!
Amazing!

God won't ask the square footage of your house, but He'll ask how many people you welcomed into your home.

God won't ask about the clothes you had in your closet, but He'll ask how many you helped to clothe.

God won't ask about your social status, but He'll ask what kind of class you displayed.

God won't ask how many material possessions you had, but He'll ask if they dictated your life.

God won't ask what you did to help yourself, but He'll ask what you did to help others.

God won't ask how many friends you had, but He'll ask how many people to whom you were a friend.

God won't ask what you did to protect your rights, but He'll ask what you did to protect the rights of others.

God won't ask in what neighborhood you lived, but He'll ask how you treated your neighbors.

God won't ask about the color of your skin, but He'll ask about the content of your character.

God won't ask how many times your deeds matched your words, but He'll ask how many times they didn't.

❋❋❋

Exciting!
Emotional!

A little girl was talking to her teacher about whales. The teacher said it was physically impossible for a whale to swallow a human because even though it was a very large mammal its throat was very small.

The little girl stated that Jonah was swallowed by a whale.

Irritated, the teacher reiterated that a whale could not swallow a human; it was physically impossible.

The little girl said, "When I get to heaven I will ask Jonah." The teacher asked, "What if Jonah went to hell?"

The little girl replied, "Then you ask him."

A Kindergarten teacher was observing her classroom of children while they drew. She would occasionally walk around to see each child's work.

As she got to one little girl who was working diligently, she asked what the drawing was?

The girl replied, "I'm drawing God.

The teacher paused and said, "But no one knows what God looks like."

Without missing a beat, or looking up from her drawing, the girl replied, "They will in a minute."

The children had all been photographed, and the teacher was trying to persuade them each to buy a copy of the group picture.

"Just think how nice it will be to look at it when you are all grown up and say, 'There's Jennifer, she's a lawyer,' or 'That's Michael. He's a doctor.'"

A small voice at the back of the room rang out, "And there's the teacher, she's dead."

179

A teacher was giving a lesson on the circulation of the blood. Trying to make the matter clearer, she said,

"Now, class, if I stood on my head, the blood, as you know, would run into it, and I would turn red in the face."

"Yes," the class said.

"Then why is it that while I am standing upright in the ordinary position the blood doesn't run into my feet?"

A little fellow shouted, "Cause your feet ain't empty."

A group of students was asked to list what they thought were the present Seven Wonders of the World. Though there was some disagreement, the following got the most votes:

1. Egypt's Great Pyramids
2. Taj Mahal
3. Grand Canyon
4. Panama Canal
5. Empire State Building
6. St. Peter's Basilica
7. China's Great Wall

While gathering the votes, the teacher noted that one quiet student hadn't turned in her paper yet, so she asked the girl if she was having trouble with her list.

The girl replied, "Yes, a little. I couldn't quite make up my mind because there were so many."

The teacher said, "Well, tell us what you have, and maybe we can help."

180

Exciting!
Emotional!

The girl hesitated, then read, "I think the Seven Wonders of the World are:
1. to see
2. to taste
3. to touch
4. to hear
She hesitated a little, and then added,
5. to feel
6. to laugh
7. and to love
The room was so full of silence you could have heard a pin drop.

Those things we overlook as simple and "ordinary" are truly wonders.

This is a gentle reminder that the most precious things in life cannot be bought.

God gave them to us.

Being happy doesn't mean everything's perfect, it just means you've decided to see beyond the imperfections.

May you always be happy and see beyond…

✺✺✺

Next time your morning seems to be going wrong and the children are slow getting dressed and you can't seem to find the car keys and you hit every traffic light, don't get mad or frustrated: instead praise God because God is at work watching over you.

After Sept. 11th, I happened to call a man on business whom I didn't know and will probably never talk to again. But on this particular day, he felt like talking.

181

Entertaining!
Amazing!

World's Funniest and Greatest E-mails

He was the head of security for a company that had invited the remaining members of another company who had been decimated by the attack on the Twin Towers to share their office space.

With his voice full of awe he told me stories of why these people were alive and their counterparts were dead. In the end, all the stories were just about the little things that happen to us.

You might know, the head of the company got in late that day because his son started kindergarten.

Another fellow was alive because it was his turn to bring donuts. There were other stories that I hope and pray will someday be gathered and put in a book.

The one that struck me was the man who put on a new pair of shoes that morning, took the various means to get to work but before he got there, he developed a blister on his foot. He stopped at a drugstore to buy a Band-Aid. That is why he is alive.

Now when I am stuck in traffic, miss an elevator, turn back to answer a ringing telephone...all the little things that annoy me...I think to myself, this is exactly where God wants me to be at this very moment.

May God continue to bless you with all those annoying things.

Pass this on to someone else, if you'd like.
There is NO LUCK attached.
If you delete this, it's okay: God's Love Is Not Dependant On E-Mail.

※※※

Exciting!
Emotional!

No one can go back and make a brand new start.

Anyone can start from now and make a brand new ending.

God didn't promise days without pain, laughter without sorrow, sun without rain, but He did promise strength for the day, comfort for the tears, and light for the way.

Disappointments are like road bumps, they slow you down a bit but you enjoy the smooth road afterwards.

Don't stay on the bumps too long. Move on!
When you feel down because you didn't get what you want, just sit tight and be happy, because God has thought of something better to give you.

When something happens to you, good or bad, consider what it means. There's a purpose to life's events, to teach you how to laugh more or not to cry too hard.

You can't make someone love you, all you can do is be someone who can be loved, the rest is up to the person to realize your worth.

It's better to lose your pride to the one you love, than to lose the one you love because of pride.

We spend too much time looking for the right person to love or finding fault with those we already love, when instead we should be perfecting the love we give.

Never abandon an old friend. You will never find one who can take their place. Friendship is like wine, it gets better as it grows older.

Entertaining!
Amazing!

❋ ❋ ❋

This is good, read and then make a decision.

Subject: God

I don't believe in Santa Claus, but I'm not going to sue somebody for singing a Ho-Ho-Ho song in December.

I don't agree with Darwin, but I didn't go out and hire a lawyer when my high school teacher taught his theory of evolution.

Life, liberty or your pursuit of happiness will not be endangered because someone says a 30-second prayer before a football game.

So what's the big deal?

It's not like somebody is up there reading the entire book of Acts.

They're just talking to a God they believe in and asking him to grant safety to the players on the field and the fans going home from the game.

"But it's a Christian prayer," some will argue.

Yes, and this is the United States of America, a country founded on Christian principles.

And we are in the Bible Belt. According to our very own phone book, Christian churches outnumber all others better than 200-to- 1.

So what would you expect—somebody chanting Hare Krishna?

If I went to a football game in Jerusalem, I would expect to hear a Jewish prayer.

If I went to a soccer game in Baghdad, I would expect to hear a Muslim prayer.

If I went to a ping pong match in China, I would expect to hear someone pray to Buddha.

And I wouldn't be offended. It wouldn't bother me one bit. When in Rome...

"But what about the atheists?" is another argument.

What about them?

Nobody is asking them to be baptized.

We're not going to pass the collection plate.

Just humor us for 30 seconds.

If that's asking too much, bring a Walkman or a pair of ear plugs.

Go to the bathroom. Visit the concession stand. Call your lawyer.

Unfortunately, one or two will make that call.

One or two will tell thousands what they can and cannot do.

I don't think a short prayer at a football game is going to shake the world's foundations.

Christians are just sick and tired of turning the other cheek while our courts strip us of all our rights.

Our parents and grandparents taught us to pray before eating, to pray before we go to sleep.

Our Bible tells us just to pray without ceasing.

Now a handful of people and their lawyers are telling us to cease praying.

God, help us.

And if that last sentence offends you, well...just sue me.

The silent majority has been silent too long...it's time we let that one or two who scream loud enough to be heard, that the vast majority don't care what they want...it is time the majority rules!

It's time we tell them, you don't have to pray...you don't have to say the pledge of allegiance, you don't have to believe in God or attend services that honor Him.

185

That is your right, and we will honor your right…but by golly you are no longer going to take our rights away…we are fighting back…and we WILL WIN! After all the God you have the right to denounce is on our side!

God bless us one and all, especially those who denounce Him…

God bless America, despite all her faults…still the greatest nation of all…

God bless our service men who are fighting to protect our right to pray and worship God…

May 2003 be the year the silent majority is heard and we put God back as the foundation of our families and institutions.

Keep looking up…In God WE Trust

If you agree with this, please pass it on. If not, delete it!!

※ ※ ※

This is a message we should consider each day, and a very wonderful way to think of people as we fold our hands in prayer!!

God Bless You

The Five Fingers of Prayer

1. Your thumb is nearest to you. Begin your prayers by praying for those closest to you. They are the easiest to remember. To pray for our loved ones is, as C.S. Lewis once said, a "sweet duty."

2. The next finger is the pointing finger. Pray for those who teach, instruct and heal. This includes teachers, doctors, and ministers. They need support and wisdom in pointing others in the right direction. Keep them in your prayers.

3. The next finger is the tallest finger. It reminds us of our leaders. Pray for the president, leaders in business and industry and administrators. These people shape our nation and guide public opinion. They need God's guidance.

Exciting!
Emotional!

4. The fourth finger is our ring finger. Surprising to many is the fact that this is our weakest finger, as any piano teacher will testify. It should remind us to pray for those who are weak, in trouble or in pain. They need your prayers day and night. You cannot pray too much for them.

5. And lastly comes our little finger; the smallest finger of all, which is where we should place ourselves in relation to God and others. As the Bible says, "The least shall be the greatest among you." The last shall be first. Your pinkie should remind you to pray for yourself.

By the time you have prayed for the other four groups, your own needs will be put into proper perspective and you will be able to pray for yourself more effectively.

Should you decide to send this to a friend, you might brighten someone's day! Pass this on to someone special…I did, with love to you. God Bless.

❀❀❀

Billy Graham's daughter was being interviewed on the Early Show and Jane Clayson asked her "How could God let something like this happen?" regarding 9-11-01. And Anne Graham gave an extremely profound and insightful response.

She said "I believe that God is deeply saddened by this, just as we are, but for years we've been telling God to get out of our schools, to get out of our government and to get out of our lives. And being the gentleman that He is, I believe that He has calmly backed out. How can we expect God to give us His blessing and His protection if we demand that He leave us alone?" (In light of recent events…terrorists attack, school shootings, etc.)

Let's see, I think it started when Madeline Murray O'Hare (she was murdered, her body was found recently) complained she didn't want any prayer in our schools, and we said "OK."

187

Entertaining!
Amazing!

Then, someone said "you better not read the Bible in school...the Bible that says thou shalt not kill, thou shalt not steal, and love your neighbor as yourself." And we said, "OK."

Then, Dr. Benjamin Spock said we shouldn't spank our children when they misbehave because their little personalities would be warped and we might damage their self-esteem. (Dr. Spock's son committed suicide.) And we said, an expert should know what he's talking about so we said "OK."

Then, someone said "teachers and principals better not discipline our children when they misbehave." And the school administrators said "no faculty member in this school better touch a student when they misbehave because we don't want any bad publicity, and we surely don't want to be sued." (there's a big difference between disciplining and touching, beating, smacking, humiliating, kicking, etc.). And we said, "OK."

Then someone said, "Let's let our daughters have abortions if they want, and they won't even have to tell their parents." And we said, "OK."

Then some wise school board member said, "Since boys will be boys and they're going to do it anyway, let's give our sons all the condoms they want, so they can have all the fun they desire, and we won't have to tell their parents they got them at school." And we said, "OK."

Then some of our top elected officials said "It doesn't matter what we do in private as long as we do our jobs." And agreeing with them, we said "It doesn't matter to me what anyone, including the President, does in private as long as I have a job and the economy is good."

And then someone said "let's print magazines with pictures of nude women and call it wholesome, down-to-earth appreciation for the beauty of the female body." And we said, "OK."

188

Exciting!
Emotional!

And then someone else took that appreciation a step further and published pictures of nude children and then stepped further still by making them available on the internet. And we said "OK, they're entitled to their free speech."

And then the entertainment industry said, "Let's make TV shows and movies that promote profanity, violence, and illicit sex. And let's record music that encourages rape, drugs, murder, suicide, and satanic themes." And we said "it's just entertainment, it has no adverse effect, and nobody takes it seriously anyway, so go right ahead."

Now we're asking ourselves why our children have no conscience, why they don't know right from wrong, and why it doesn't bother them to kill strangers, their classmates, and themselves.

Probably, if we think about it long and hard enough, we can figure it out. I think it has a great deal to do with "WE REAP WHAT WE SOW."

"Dear God, Why didn't you save the little girl killed in her classroom?" Sincerely, Concerned Student…AND THE REPLY "Dear Concerned Student, I am not allowed in schools." Sincerely, God.

Funny how simple it is for people to trash God and then wonder why the world's going to hell. Funny how we believe what the newspapers say, but question what the Bible says.

Funny how everyone wants to go to heaven provided they do not have to believe, think, say, or do anything the Bible says.

Funny how someone can say "I believe in God" but still follow Satan who, by the way, also "believes" in God.

189

Entertaining!
Amazing!

Funny how we are quick to judge but not to be judged.

Funny how you can send a thousand 'jokes' through e-mail and they spread like wildfire, but when you start sending messages regarding the Lord, people think twice about sharing.

Funny how the lewd, crude, vulgar and obscene pass freely through cyberspace, but the public discussion of God is suppressed in the school and workplace.

Funny how someone can be so fired up for Christ on Sunday, but be an invisible Christian the rest of the week.

Are you laughing?

Funny how when you go to forward this message, you will not send it to many on your address list because you're not sure what they believe, or what they will think of you for sending it to them. Funny how I can be more worried about what other people think of me than what God thinks of me.

Are you thinking?

Pass it on if you think it has merit. If not then just discard it…no one will know that you did. But, if you discard this thought process, then don't sit back and complain about what bad shape the world is in!

※※※

Our house was directly across the street from the clinic entrance of Johns Hopkins Hospital in Baltimore. We lived downstairs and rented the upstairs rooms to out patients at the clinic.

One summer evening as I was fixing supper, there was a knock at the door. I opened it to see a truly awful looking man. "Why, he's hardly taller than my eight-year old," I thought as I stared at the stooped, shriveled body. But the appalling thing was his face, lopsided from swelling, red and raw. Yet his voice was pleasant as he said, "Good evening. I've come to see if you've a room for just one night. I came for a treatment this morning from the eastern shore, and there's no bus 'til morning."

He told me he'd been hunting for a room since noon but with no success, no one seemed to have a room. "I guess it's my face…I know it looks terrible, but my doctor says with a few more treatments…"

For a moment I hesitated, but his next words convinced me: "I could sleep in this rocking chair on the porch. My bus leaves early in the morning."

I told him we would find him a bed, but to rest on the porch. I went inside and finished getting supper. When we were ready, I asked the old man if he would join us. "No thank you. I have plenty."

And he held up a brown paper bag.

When I had finished the dishes, I went out on the porch to talk with him a few minutes. It didn't take a long time to see that this old man had an oversized heart crowded into that tiny body. He told me he fished for a living to support his daughter, her five children, and her husband, who was hopelessly crippled from a back injury.

He didn't tell it by way of complaint; in fact, every other sentence was preface with a thanks to God for a blessing. He was grateful that no pain accompanied his disease, which was apparently a form of skin cancer. He thanked God for giving him the strength to keep going.

191

@ntertaining!
@mazing!

At bedtime, we put a camp cot in the children's room for him. When I got up in the morning, the bed linens were neatly folded and the little man was out on the porch.

He refused breakfast, but just before he left for his bus, haltingly, as if asking a great favor, he said, "Could I please come back and stay the next time I have a treatment? I won't put you out a bit. I can sleep fine in a chair." He paused a moment and then added, "Your children made me feel at home. Grownups are bothered by my face, but children don't seem to mind." I told him he was welcome to come again.

On his next trip he arrived a little after seven in the morning. As a gift, he brought a big fish and a quart of the largest oysters I had ever seen. He said he had shucked them that morning before he left that they'd be nice and fresh. I knew his bus left at 4:00 a.m. and I wondered what time he had to get up in order to do this for us.

In the years he came to stay overnight with us there was never a time that he did not bring us fish or oysters or vegetables from his garden.

Other times we received packages in the mail, always by special delivery; fish and oysters packed in a box of fresh young spinach or kale, every leaf carefully washed. Knowing that he must walk three miles to mail these, and knowing how little money he had made the gifts doubly precious.

When I received these little remembrances, I often thought of a comment our next-door neighbor made after he left that first morning.

"Did you keep that awful looking man last night? I turned him away! You can lose roomers by putting up such people!"

Maybe we did lose roomers once or twice. But oh! If only they could have known him, perhaps their illness' would have been easier to bear. I know our family always will be grateful to have known him. From him, we learned what it was to accept the bad without complaint and the good with gratitude to God.

192

Exciting!
Emotional!

Recently I was visiting a friend who has a greenhouse. As she showed me her flowers, we came to the most beautiful one of all, a golden chrysanthemum, bursting with blooms. But to my great surprise, it was growing in an old dented, rusty bucket. I thought to myself, "If this were my plant, I'd put it in the loveliest container I had!"

My friend changed my mind. "I ran short of pots," she explained, and knowing how beautiful this one would be, I thought it wouldn't mind starting out in this old pail. It's just for a little while, till I can put it out in the garden."

She must have wondered why I laughed so delightedly, but I was imagining just such a scene in heaven. "Here's an especially beautiful one," God might have said when he came to the soul of the sweet old fisherman. "He won't mind starting in this small body."

All this happened long ago – and now, in God's garden, how tall this lovely soul must stand.

The LORD does not look at the things man looks at. Man looks at the outward appearance, but the LORD looks at the heart." (1 Samuel 16:7b)

Friends are very special. They make you smile and encourage you to succeed. They lend an ear and they share a word of praise.

World's Funniest and Greatest E-mails

exciting!
emotional!

Chapter 6

Something to Offend Everyone

Part I

What do you call two Mexicans playing basketball?
Juan on Juan.

What is a Yankee?
The same as a quickie, but a guy can do it alone.

What is the difference between a Harley and a Hoover?
The position of the dirt bag.

Why is divorce so expensive?
Because it's worth it.

Why is air a lot like sex?
Because it's no big deal unless you're not getting any.

Something to offend everyone part II (just warming up!)

What do you call a smart blonde?
A golden retriever.

What do attorneys use for birth control?
Their personalities.

What's the difference between a girlfriend and wife?
45 lbs.

What's the difference between a boyfriend and husband?
45 minutes.

Exciting!
Emotional!

What's the fastest way to a man's heart?
Through his chest with a sharp knife.

Why do men want to marry virgins?
They can't stand criticism.

Why is it so hard for women to find men that are sensitive, caring, and good-looking?
Because those men already have boyfriends.

What's the difference between a new husband and a new dog?
After a year, the dog is still excited to see you.

What makes men chase women they have no intention of marrying?
The same urge that makes dogs chase cars they have no intention of driving.

Why don't bunnies make noise when they have sex?
Because they have cotton balls.

What did the blonde say when she found out she was pregnant?
"Are you sure it's mine?"

Why does Mike Tyson cry during sex?
Mace will do that to you.

Why did OJ Simpson want to move to West Virginia?
Everyone has the same DNA.

Why do men find it difficult to make eye contact?
Breasts don't have eyes.

197

Did you hear about the dyslexic Rabbi?
He walks around saying "Yo."

Why do drivers' education classes in Redneck schools use the car only on Mondays, Wednesdays and Fridays?
Because on Tuesday and Thursday, the Sex Ed class uses it.

Something to offend everyone, part III (just great stuff)

Where does an Irish family go on vacation?
A different bar.

Did you hear about the Chinese couple that had a retarded baby?
They named him "Sum Ting Wong"

What would you call it when an Italian has one arm shorter than the other?
A speech impediment.

What does it mean when the flag at the Post Office is flying at half-mast?
They're hiring.

What's the difference between a southern zoo and a northern zoo?
A southern zoo has a description of the animal on the front of the cage along with "a recipe".

How do you get a sweet little 80-year-old lady to say the "F" word?
Get another sweet little 80-year-old lady to yell *BINGO*!

What's the difference between a Northern fairytale and a Southern fairytale?
A Northern fairytale begins "Once upon a time..." A Southern fairytale begins "Y'all ain't gonna believe this shit..."

Exciting!
Emotional!

Why is there no Disneyland in China?
No one's tall enough to go on the good rides.

✸✸✸

A construction boss in Boston was interviewing men when along came a guy named Vinny from New York. "I'm not hiring any wise-ass New Yorker," the fore-man thought, so he made up a test hoping that Vinny wouldn't be able to answer the questions, and he'd be able to refuse him the job without getting into a dispute.

"Here's your first question," the foreman said.

"Without using numbers, represent the number 9."

"Widout numbiz?" Vinny says.

"Dat's easy," and he proceeds to draw 3 trees.

"What's this?" the boss asks.

The New Yorker replies, "Ain't you got no brains?

Tree 'n Tree 'n Tree makes nine. Faghedaboutit..."

"Fair enough," says the Boss. "Here's your second question.

Use the same rules, but this time use the number 99."

Vinny stares into space for a minute, then picks up the picture he has drawn and makes a smudge on each tree. "Dare ya go, Buddy."

The Boss scratches his head and says, "How on earth do you get that to repre-sent 99?"

Vinny says "Each a da tree's is dirty now! So it's dirty tree 'n dirty tree 'n dirty tree-dat's 99".

The Boss is getting worried he's going to have to hire the New Yorker, so he says, "All right, last question. Same rules but this time use 100."

Entertaining!
Amazing!

Vinny stares into space again, then picks up the picture once again, makes a little mark at the base of each tree and says, "Dare ya go, Mac, a hunnert."

The Boss looks at the picture for a moment and says, "You must be nuts if you think that represents 100!"

New York Vinny leans forward and points to the marks at the base of the trees. "A little doggie comes along and takes a shit on each a dem trees, so now ya got dirty tree an' a turd, dirty tree an' a turd, dirty tree an' a turd – which makes one hundred. Bada boom, bada bing. When do I freakin' start?"

☀ ☀ ☀

Just in case you plan on a trip to Texas!

Two men are driving through Texas when they get pulled over by a State Trooper. The cop walks up and taps on the window with his nightstick…

The driver rolls down the window and WHACK, the cop smacks him in the head with the stick. The driver asks, "What the hell was that for?" The cop answers, "You're in Texas, son. When we pull you over, you better have your license ready when we get to your car." The driver says, "I'm sorry, Officer, I'm not from around here." The cop runs a check on the guy's license, and he's clean. He gives the guy his license back, walks around to the passenger side and taps on the window!

The passenger rolls down the window and WHACK, the cop smacks him on the head with the nightstick…The passenger asks, "What'd you do that for?" The cop says, "Just making your wish come true." The passenger asks, "Making what wish come true?" The cop says, "I know that two miles down the road you're gonna say to your buddy here, "I wish that asshole would've tried that shit with me!"

200

※※※

"The unfair thing about life is the way it ends. I mean, life is tough.

It takes up a lot of your time. What do you get at the end of it? Death. What's that, a bonus? I think the life cycle is all backwards.

You should die first, get it out of the way.

Then you live in an old age home.

You get kicked out when you're too young, you get a gold watch, you go to work. You work forty years until you're young enough to enjoy your retirement.

You do drugs, alcohol, you party, and you get ready for high school.

You go to grade school, you become a kid, you play, you have no responsibilities, you become a little baby, you go back into the womb, you spend your last nine months floating...

...you finish off as an orgasm."

※※※

Two friends, a white guy and a black guy, both work together. The white guy came in late one morning and his black friend asks where he had been.

The white guy says, "My wife gives me good sex every night and she kept me up really late last night".

The black guy says "I can't get my wife to have sex with me, no matter what! How do you do it?"

The white guy says, "I read her poetry every night."

His black friend then asks, "What kind of poetry?"

Entertaining!
Amazing!

The white guy replies, "Blondie, blondie, eyes so blue, how I want to make love to you." Then the white guy tells his friend to go home and try it – it's a sure thing!

The next morning the black guy was about two hours late. When he comes in, he has a black eye and his arm is in a sling.

The white man asks, "What happened?!"

The black man says, "Man, don't ever speak to me again!"

The curious white man asks, "Well, what did you say to her?"

The black man replies, "Nappy head, nappy head, eyes like a frog, bend over bitch, and take it like a dog!!"

☀ ☀ ☀

Five surgeons are discussing who makes the best patients to operate on.

The first surgeon says, "I like to see accountants on my operating table, because when you open them up, everything inside is numbered."

The second responds, "Yeah, but you should try electricians. Everything inside them is color-coded."

The third surgeon says, "No, I really think librarians are the best. Everything inside them is in alphabetical order."

The fourth surgeon chimes in: "You know, I like mechanics. They always understand when you have a few parts left over at the end and when the job takes longer than you said it would."

But the fifth surgeon shuts them all up when he observes: "The French are the easiest to operate on. There's no guts, no heart, no balls and no spine. Plus the head and ass are interchangeable."

202

✸✸✸

An airline's passenger cabin was being served by an obviously gay flight attendant, who seemed to put everyone into a good mood as he served them food and drinks.

As the plane prepared to descend, he came swishing down the aisle and announced to the passengers, "Captain Marvey has asked me to announce that he'll be landing the big scary plane shortly, lovely people, so if you could just put up your trays that would be super."

On his trip back up the aisle, he noticed that a well-dressed rather exotic looking woman hadn't moved a muscle. "Perhaps you didn't hear me over those big brute engines. I asked you to raise your trazy-poo so the main man can pitty-pat us on the ground."

She calmly turned her head and said, "In my country, I am called a Princess. I take orders from no one." To which the flight attendant replied, without missing a beat, "Well, sweet-cheeks, in my country, I'm called a Queen, so I outrank you. Tray-up bitch."

✸✸✸

These questions about Australia were posted on an Australian Tourism Website and obviously the answers came from a fellow Aussie.

1. Q: Does it ever get windy in Australia? I have never seen it rain on TV, so how do the plants grow? (UK)
A: We import all plants fully grown and then just sit around watching them die.

2. Q: Will I be able to see kangaroos in the street? (USA)
A: Depends how much you've been drinking

Entertaining!
Amazing!

3. Q: I want to walk from Perth to Sydney – can I follow the railroad tracks? (Sweden)

A: Sure, it's only three thousand miles, take lots of water…

4. Q: Is it safe to run around in the bushes in Australia? (Sweden)

A: So its true what they say about Swedes.

5. Q: It is imperative that I find the names and addresses of places to contact for a stuffed porpoise. (Italy)

A: Let's not touch this one.

6. Q: Are there any ATMs (cash machines) in Australia? Can you send me a list of them in Brisbane, Cairns, Townsville and Hervey Bay? (UK)

A: What did your last slave die of?

7. Q: Can you give me some information about hippo racing in Australia? (USA)

A: A-fri-ca is the big triangle shaped continent south of Europe. Aus-tra-lia is that big island in the middle of the Pacific which does not…oh forget it. Sure, the hippo racing is every Tuesday night in Kings Cross. Come naked.

8. Q: Which direction is North in Australia? (USA)

A: Face south and then turn 90 degrees. Contact us when you get here and we'll send the rest of the directions.

9. Q: Can I bring cutlery into Australia? (UK)

A: Why? Just use your fingers like we do.

10. Q: Can you send me the Vienna Boys' Choir schedule? (USA)

A: Aus-tri-a is that quaint little country bordering Ger-man-y, which is…oh forget it. Sure, the Vienna Boys Choir plays every Tuesday night in Kings Cross, straight after the hippo races. Come naked.

11. Q: Do you have perfume in Australia? (France)

A: No, WE don't stink.

12. Q: I have developed a new product that is the fountain of youth. Can you tell me where I can sell it in Australia? (USA)

A: Anywhere significant numbers of Americans gather.

13. Q: Can I wear high heels in Australia? (UK)

A: You are a British politician, right?

14. Q: Can you tell me the regions in Tasmania where the female population is smaller than the male population? (Italy)

A: Yes, gay nightclubs.

15. Q: Do you celebrate Christmas in Australia? (France)

A: Only at Christmas.

17. Q: Are there supermarkets in Sydney and is milk available all year round? (Germany)

A: No, we are a peaceful civilisation of vegan hunter gatherers. Milk is illegal.

205

Entertaining!
Amazing!

18. Q: Please send a list of all doctors in Australia who can dispense rattle-snake serum. (USA)

A: Rattlesnakes live in A-meri-ca which is where YOU come from. All Australian snakes are perfectly harmless, can be safely handled and make good pets.

19. Q: I have a question about a famous animal in Australia, but I forget its name. It's a kind of bear and lives in trees. (USA)

A: It's called a Drop Bear. They are so called because they drop out of gum trees and eat the brains of anyone walking underneath them. You can scare them off by spraying yourself with human urine before you go out walking.

21. Q: I was in Australia in 1969 on R+R, and I want to contact the girl I dated while I was staying in Kings Cross. Can you help? (USA)

A: Yes, and you will still have to pay her by the hour.

22. Q: Will I be able to speak English most places I go? (USA)

A: Yes, but you'll have to learn it first.

❋❋❋

Subject: Good Ole Irish

Into a Belfast pub comes Paddy Murphy, looking like he'd just been run over by a train. His arm is in a sling, his nose is broken, his face is cut and bruised and he's walking with a limp. "What happened to you?" asks Sean, the bartender. "Jamie O'Conner and me had a fight," says Paddy. "That little shit, O'Conner," says Sean, "He couldn't do that to you, he must have had something in his hand." "That he did," says Paddy, "a shovel is what he had, and a terrible lickin' he gave me with it." "Well," says Sean, "you should have defended yourself, didn't you

206

Exciting! Emotional!

have something in your hand?" "That I did," said Paddy. "Mrs. O'Conner's breast, and a thing of beauty it was, but useless in a fight."

An Irishman who had a little too much to drink is driving home from the city one night and, of course, his car is weaving violently all over the road. A cop pulls him over. "So," says the cop to the driver, where have ya been?" "Why, I've been to the pub of course," slurs the drunk. "Well," says the cop, "it looks like you've had quite a few to drink this evening." "I did all right," the drunk says with a smile. "Did you know," says the cop, standing straight and folding his arms across his chest, "that a few intersections back, your wife fell out of your car?" "Oh, thank heavens," sighs the drunk. "For a minute there, I thought I'd gone deaf."

Brenda O'Malley is home making dinner, as usual, when Tim Finnegan arrives at her door. "Brenda, may I come in?" he asks. "I've somethin' to tell ya." "Of course you can come in, you're always welcome, Tim. But where's my husband?" "That's what I'm here to be tellin' ya, Brenda. "There was an accident down at the Guinness brewery…" "Oh, God no!" cries Brenda. "Please don't tell me…" "I must, Brenda. Your husband Shamus is dead and gone. I'm sorry." Finally, she looked up at Tim. "How did it happen, Tim?" "It was terrible, Brenda. He fell into a vat of Guinness Stout and drowned." "Oh my dear Jesus! But you must tell me true, Tim. "Did he at least go quickly?" "Well, no Brenda…no. Fact is, he got out three times to pee."

Mary Clancy goes up to Father O'Grady after his Sunday morning service, and she's in tears. He says, "So what's bothering you, Mary my dear?" She says, "Oh, Father, I've got terrible news. My husband passed away last night." The priest says,

Entertaining!
Amazing!

"Oh, Mary, that's terrible. Tell me, Mary, did he have any last requests?" She says, "That he did, Father…" The priest says, "What did he ask, Mary?" She says, "He said, 'Please Mary, put down that damn gun…'"

AND THE BEST FOR LAST. A drunk staggers into a Catholic Church, enters a confessional booth, sits down but says nothing. The Priest coughs a few times to get his attention but the drunk just sits there. Finaly, the Priest pounds three times on the wall. The drunk mumbles, "ain't no use knockin, there's no paper on this side either".

☀ ☀ ☀

The French

"France has neither winter nor summer nor morals. Apart from these drawbacks it is a fine country. France has usually been governed by prostitutes." —Mark Twain

"I just love the French. They taste like chicken!"— Hannibal Lecter

While speaking to the Hoover Institution today, Secretary Donald Rumsfeld was asked this question: "Could you tell us why to date at least the Administration doesn't favor direct talks with the North Korean government? After all, we're talking with the French."
The Secretary smiled and replied: "I'm not going there!"

"I would rather have a German division in front of me than a French one behind me."—General George S. Patton

208

"Going to war without France is like going deer hunting without your accordian."—Norman Schwartzkopf

"We can stand here like the French, or we can do something about it."—Marge Simpson

"As far as I'm concerned, war always means failure."—Jacques Chirac, President of France

"As far as France is concerned, you're right."—Rush Limbaugh

"The only time France wants us to go to war is when the German Army is sitting in Paris sipping coffee."—Regis Philbin

☀☀☀

There was a Frenchman, an Englishman and Claudia Schiffer sitting together in a carriage in a train going through Provence. Suddenly the train went through a tunnel and as it was an old style train, there were no lights in the carriages and it went completely dark. Then there was a kissing noise and the sound of a really loud slap. When the train came out of the tunnel, Claudia Schiffer and the Englishman were sitting as if nothing had happened and the Frenchman had his hand against his face as if he had been slapped there. The Frenchman was thinking: 'The English fella must have kissed Claudia Schiffer and she missed him and slapped me instead.' Claudia Schiffer was thinking: 'The French fella must have tried to kiss me and actually kissed the Englishman and got slapped for it.' And the Englishman was thinking: 'This is great. The next time the train goes through a tunnel I'll make another kissing noise and slap that French bastard again.'

209

Entertaining!
Amazing!

✹✹✹

"The French are a smallish, monkey-looking bunch and not dressed any better, on average, than the citizens of Baltimore. True, you can sit outside in Paris and drink little cups of coffee, but why this is more stylish than sitting inside and drinking large glasses of whiskey I don't know."—P.J O'Rourke (1989)

Next time there's a war in Europe, the loser has to keep France.

An old saying: Raise your right hand if you like the French…Raise both hands if you are French.

"You know, the French remind me a little bit of an aging actress of the 1940s who was still trying to dine out on her looks but doesn't have the face for it."—John McCain, U.S. Senator from Arizona

"You know why the French don't want to bomb Saddam Hussein? Because he hates America, he loves mistresses and wears a beret. He is French, people." —Conan O'Brien

"I don't know why people are surprised that France won't help us get Saddam out of Iraq. After all, France wouldn't help us get the Germans out of France!" —Jay Leno

"The last time the French asked for 'more proof' it came marching into Paris under a German flag."—David Letterman

✹✹✹

@xciting!
@motional!

Replacements for the French National Anthem:

"Runaway" by Del Shannon,
"Walk Right In" by the Rooftop Singers,
"Everybody's Somebody's Fool" by Connie Francis,
"Running Scared" by Roy Orbison,
"I Really Don't Want to Know" by Tommy Edwards,
"Surrender" by Elvis Presley,
"Save It For Me" by The Four Seasons,
"Live and Let Die" by Wings,
"I'm Leaving It All Up To You" by Donny and Marie Osmond,
"What a Fool Believes" by the Doobie Brothers,
"Don't Worry, Be Happy" by Bobby McFerrin
"Raise Your Hands" by Jon Bon Jovi

How many Frenchmen does it take to change a light bulb? One. He holds the bulb and all of Europe revolves around him.

☀☀☀

A bus stops and two Italian men get on.
They sit down and engage in an animated conversation.
The lady sitting behind them ignores them at first, but her attention is galvanized when she hears one of the men say the following "Emma come first.
Den I come.
Den two asses come together.
I come once-a-more.
Two asses, they come together again.
I come again and pee twice.

211

Entertaining!
Amazing!

Then I come one lasta time."

"You foul-mouthed sex obsessed swine," retorted the lady indignantly. "In this…

"Hey, coola down lady," said the man.

"Who talkin' abouta sexa?

I'm a justa tellin' my frienda how to spella 'Mississippi'."

I BET YOU READ THIS AGAIN!!!

☀☀☀

The teacher walks in and finds an apple on her desk with the letters "ILU" written on it. She asks who left the apple, and a little white girl raises her hand.

"Well, sweetie, what does 'ILU' mean?" The little girl replies, "I love you."

The teacher says, "Isn't that sweet" and continues with class.

The next day the teacher finds a banana on her desk with the letters "YAS" written on it. The teacher asks who left the banana and what the letters mean.

A little brown girl raises her hand and says, "It means, 'You are special.'"

"Thank you sweetheart," the teacher says.

The following day, the teacher walks in to find a watermelon with the letters "FUCK" written on it. The enraged teacher asks who left it.

A little black boy raises his hand and cheerfully says, "Yes ma'am, I left it."

"It means, From Us Colored Kids."

☀☀☀

Exciting!
Emotional!

Ole, Lars and Sven

Three Norwegians, Ole, Lars and Sven, had been going to the Sons of Norway hall meetings as long as there had been a hall. And every month, wouldn't ya know it, they never won a prize at the monthly drawing. That is, until last meeting.

Sven was the first one of the three to have his name drawn. He won two pounds of spaghetti sauce, four boxes of noodles and three pounds of Swedish meatballs.

Ole had his name drawn next. He got himself round trip tickets to Duluth, MN., two nights' stay at the Dew Drop Inn, and a pair of tickets to see the Inger Triplets Polka Ensemble. Ole thought that he had died and gone to heaven.

Lars was the last one to have his name drawn. He won a toilet brush.

At the next monthly meeting, they sat down together to check out how they had fared for the past month. Sven said, "Uff da, I had dat pasghetti for tree days. It was so good, and Helga didn't have to buy food for dem dere tree days."

Ole said, "Lena was so happy vhen I brought home dem tickets. The trip up to Duloot was nice, and we got to ride da Greyhound, and you know, they got a built-in outhouse on dat dere bus. And the Inger Triplets, if I didn't know better, I would swear dey vere sisters."

Then Ole turned to Lars, and asked him how his prize worked out. Lars looked at them both and said, "Dat dere toilet brush is nice, but I tink I'll go back to using paper.

❅❅❅

Oakland Quarterback

The Coach had put together the perfect team for the Oakland Raiders. The only thing that was missing was a good quarterback. He had scouted all the colleges, and even the high schools, but he couldn't find a ringer quarterback who

213

Entertaining!
Amazing!

could ensure a Super Bowl win. Then one night, while watching CNN, he saw a war-zone scene in Afghanistan.

In one corner of the background, he spotted a young Afghanistan Soldier with a truly incredible arm. He threw a hand grenade straight into a 3rd story window 200 yards away, ka-boom! He threw another hand grenade into a group of 10 soldiers 100 yards away, ka-blooey! Then a car passed, going 90 mph, he throws the grenade at the car and it went in to the open window. Bulls eye!

"I've got to get this guy!" the coach said to himself. "He has the perfect arm!"

So, he brings him to the United States and teaches him the great game of football, and the Raiders go on to win the Super Bowl the very next season.

The young Afghani is hailed as the Great Hero of football, and when the Coach asks him what he wants, all the young man wants to do is to call his mother.

"Mom," he says into the phone, "I just won the Super Bowl!"

"I don't want to talk to you," the old woman says. "You deserted us. You are not my son."

"I don't think you understand, Mother!" the young man pleads. "I just won the greatest sporting event in the world. I'm here among thousands of my adoring fans."

"No, let me tell you," his mother retorts. "At this very moment, there are gunshots all around us. The neighborhood is a pile of rubble. Your two brothers were beaten within an inch of their lives last week, and this week your sister was raped in broad daylight."

The old lady pauses, and then tearfully says, "I'll never forgive you for making us move to Oakland."

※※※

214

Exciting!
Emotional!

Chapter 6. Something to Offend Everyone

One beautiful December evening Huan Cho and his girlfriend Jung Lee were sitting on a beach by the ocean. It was a romantic full moon, when Huan Cho said "Hey baby, let's play Weeweechu."

"Oh no, not now, lets look at the moon" said Jung Lee.

"Oh, c'mon baby, let's you and I play Weeweechu. I love you and its the perfect time," Huan Cho begged.

"But I rather just hold your hand and watch the moon."

"Please Jung Lee, just once play Weeweechu with me."

Jung Lee looked at Huan Chi and said, "OK, we'll play Weeweechu."

Huan Cho grabbed his guitar and they both sang...

"Weeweechu a Merry Christmas
Weeweechu a Merry Christmas,
Weeweechu a Merry Christmas and a Happy New Year."

(Ha! And you thought this was going to be naughty!)

✹✹✹

When I born, I black.
When I grow up, I black.
When I go in sun, I black.
When I cold, I black.
When I scared, I black.
When I sick, I black.
And when I die, I still black.
You white folks: When you born, you pink.
When you grow up, you white.
When you go in sun, you red.

215

Entertaining!
Amazing!

When you cold, you blue.
When you scared, you yellow.
When you sick, you green.
When you bruised, you purple.
And when you die, you gray.
So who you callin' colored.

☀☀☀

Dayvorce...

A farmer who wanted to get a divorce paid a visit to a lawyer.
The lawyer said, "How can I help you?"
The farmer said, "I want to get one of those dayvorces".
The lawyer said, "Do you have any grounds?"
The farmer said, "Yes, I got 40 acres".
The lawyer said, "No, you don't understand, Do you have a suit?"
The farmer said, "Yes, I got a suit, I wears it to church on Sundays".
The lawyer said, "No, no, I mean, do you have a case?"
The farmer said, "No, I ain't got a case, but I got a John Deere."
The lawyer said, "No, I mean, do you have a grudge?"
The farmer said, "Yes, I got a grudge, That's where I parks the John Deere."
The lawyer said, "Does your wife beat you up or something?"
The farmer said, "No, we both get up at 4:30".
The lawyer said, "Is your wife a nagger?".
The farmer said, "No, she's a little white gal, but our last child was a nagger and that's why I wants a dayvorce."

☀☀☀

216

Exciting!
Emotional!

Bubba Died in a Fire

Bubba died in a fire and his body was burned pretty badly. The morgue needed someone to identify the body, so they sent for his two best friends, Daryl and Gomer. The three men had always done everything together.

Daryl arrived first, and when the mortician pulled back the sheet, Daryl said, "Yup, his face is burnt up pretty bad. You better roll him over."

The mortician rolled him over and Daryl said, "Nope, ain't Bubba."

The mortician thought that was rather strange. Then he brought Gomer in to identify the body. Gomer took a look at the body and said, "Yup, he's pretty well burnt up. Roll him over."

The mortician rolled him over and Gomer said, "No, it ain't Bubba."

The mortician asked, "How can you tell?"

Gomer said, "Well, Bubba had two assholes."

"What? He had two assholes?!" said the mortician.

"Yup, everyone knew he had two assholes. Every time we went to town, folks would say, 'Here comes Bubba with them two assholes.'"

❋❋❋

Subject: Leroy

An Arkansas woman is in the welfare office filling out forms. The welfare officer asks her how many children she has.

The woman replies, "Ten boys." The welfare officer asked, "What are their names?" The woman said, "Leroy, Leroy, Leroy, Leroy, Leroy, Leroy, Leroy, Leroy, Leroy and Leroy."

After the surprised look wore off of the welfare officer's face she asked, "All named Leroy? Why would you name them all Leroy?"

217

Entertaining!
Amazing!

The woman said, "That way, when I wants them all to come in from the yard I just yells LEROY, and when I wants them all to come to dinner I just yells LEROY!"

The welfare officer asked, "What if you just want a particular one of them to do something?"

"Then I calls him by his last name," the woman responded.

☀ ☀ ☀

An Irishman named O'Malley went to his doctor after a long illness. The doctor, after a lengthy examination, sighed and looked O'Malley in the eye and said, "I've some bad news for your, you have cancer, and it can't be cured. You'd best put your affairs in order."

O'Malley was shocked and saddened. But, being of solid character, he managed to compose himself and walk from the doctor's office into the waiting room.

To his son who had been waiting, O'Malley said, "Well, son, we Irish celebrate when things are good and we celebrate when things don't go so well. In this case, things aren't so well. I have cancer. Let's head for the pub and have a few pints."

After three or four pints, the two were feeling a little less somber. There were some laughs and more beers. They were eventually approached by some of O'Malley's old friends who asked what the two were celebrating. O'Malley told them that the Irish celebrate the good and the bad. He went on to tell them that they were drinking to his impending end. He told his friends, "I have been diagnosed with AIDS."

The friends gave O'Malley their condolences, and they had a couple more beers. After his friends left, O'Malley's son leaned over and whispered his confusion. "Dad, I thought you said that you were dying from cancer? You just told your friends that you were dying from AIDS!" O'Malley said, "I don't want any of them sleeping with your mother after I'm gone."

Exciting!
Emotional!

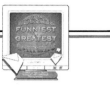

Chapter 7

Hmmm...

Since many of us have paid into FICA for years and are now receiving a Social Security check every month – and then finding that we are getting taxed on 85% of the money we paid to the federal government to "put away," you may be interested in the following:

Q: Which party took Social Security from an independent fund and put it in the general fund so that Congress could spend it?
A: It was Lyndon Johnson and the Democratic-controlled House and Senate.

Q: Which party put a tax on Social Security?
A: The Democratic party.

Q: Which party increased the tax on Social Security?
A: The Democratic Party with Al Gore casting the deciding vote.

Q: Which party decided to give money to immigrants?
A: That's right, immigrants moved into this country and at 65 got SSI Social Security. The Democratic Party gave that to them although they never paid a dime into it.

Then, after doing all this, the Democrats turn around and tell you the Republicans want to take your Social Security.

And the worst part about it is, people believe it!

2004 Election Issue

This must be an issue in "04." Please! Keep it going. Perhaps we are asking the wrong questions during election years. Our Senators and Congressmen and women do not pay into Social Security and, of course, they do not collect from it.

Exciting!
Emotional!

You see, Social Security benefits were not suitable for persons of their rare elevation in society. They felt they should have a special plan for themselves. So, many years ago they voted in their own benefit plan.

In more recent years, no congressperson has felt the need to change it. After all, it is a great plan.

For all practical purposes their plan works like this: When they retire, they continue to draw the same pay until they die, except it may increase from time to time for cost of living adjustments.

For example, former Senator Byrd and Congressman White and their wives may expect to draw $7,800,000.00 (that's Seven Million, Eight-Hundred Thousand Dollars), with their wives drawing $275,000.00 during the last years of their lives. This is calculated on an average life span for each.

Their cost for this excellent plan is $00.00. Nada. Zilch. This little perk they voted for themselves is free to them. You and I pick up the tab for this plan. The funds for this fine retirement plan come directly from the General Funds – our tax dollars at work!

From our own Social Security Plan, which you and I pay (or have paid) into every payday until we retire (which amount is matched by our employer) – we can expect to get an average $1,000 per month after retirement. Or, in other words, we would have to collect our average of $1,000. monthly benefits for 68 years and one (1) month to equal former Senator Bill Bradley's benefits!

Social Security could be very good if only one small change were made.

That change would be to jerk the Golden Fleece Retirement Plan from under the Senators and Congressmen. Put them into the Social Security plan with the rest of us…then sit back and watch how fast they would fix it.

221

Entertaining!
Amazing!

If enough people receive this, maybe a seed of awareness will be planted and maybe good changes will evolve.

How many people can YOU send this to?

❈ ❈ ❈

You Live in California when...

1. You make over $250,000 and you still can't afford to buy a house.
2. The high school quarterback calls a time-out to answer his cell phone.
3. The fastest part of your commute is going down your driveway.
4. You know how to eat an artichoke.
5. You drive your rented Mercedes to your neighborhood block party.
6. When someone asks you how far something is, you tell them how long it will take to get there rather than how many miles away it is.

You Live in New York City when...

1. You say "the city" and expect everyone to know you mean Manhattan.
2. You have never been to the Statue of Liberty or the Empire State Building.
3. You can get into a four-hour argument about how to get from Columbus Circle to Battery Park, but can't find Wisconsin on a map.
4. You think Central Park is "nature,"
5. You believe that being able to swear at people in their own language makes you multi-lingual.
6. You've worn out a car horn.
7. You think eye contact is an act of aggression.

222

Exciting!
Emotional!

Chapter 7. Hmmm...

You Live in Maine when…

    1. You only have four spices: salt, pepper, ketchup, and Tabasco.

    2. Halloween costumes fit over parkas.

    3. You have more than one recipe for moose.

    4. Sexy lingerie is anything flannel with less than eight buttons.

    5. The four seasons are: winter, still winter, almost winter, and construction.

You Live in the Deep South when…

    1. You can rent a movie and buy bait in the same store.

    2. "ya'll" is singular and "all ya'll" is plural.

    3. After five years you still hear, "You ain't from 'round here, are Ya?"

    4. "He needed killin'" is a valid defense.

    5. Everyone has two first names: Billy Bob, Jimmy Bob, Mary Sue, Betty Jean, Mary Beth, etc.

You live in Colorado when…

    1. You carry your $3,000 mountain bike atop your $500 car.

    2. You tell your husband to pick up Granola on his way home and he stops at the day care center.

    3. A pass does not involve a football or dating.

    4. The top of your head is bald, but you still have a pony tail.

You live in the Midwest when…

    1. You've never met any celebrities, but the mayor knows your name.

    2. Your idea of a traffic jam is ten cars waiting to pass a tractor.

☀ ☀ ☀

Entertaining!
Amazing!

An Amazing Conclusion

1. The sport of choice for the urban poor is BASKETBALL.
2. The sport of choice for maintenance level employees is BOWLING.
3. The sport of choice for front-line workers is FOOTBALL.
4. The sport of choice for supervisors is BASEBALL.
5. The sport of choice for middle management is TENNIS.
6. The sport of choice for corporate officers is GOLF.

AMAZING CONCLUSION:

The higher you are in the corporate structure, the smaller your balls become.

✸✸✸

Rules of Life

Sometimes we need to remember WHAT the Rules of Life really are.

1. Never give yourself a haircut after three alcoholic beverages of any kind.
2. You need only two tools: WD-40 and duct tape. If it doesn't move and it should, use WD-40. If it moves and shouldn't, use the tape.
3. The five most essential words for a healthy, vital relationship are "I apologize" and "You are right."
4. Everyone seems normal until you get to know them.
5. When you make a mistake, make amends immediately. It's easier to eat crow while it's still warm.
6. The only really good advice that your mother ever gave you was: "Go! You might meet somebody!"
7. If he/she says that you are too good for him/her – believe them.

8. Learn to pick your battles. Ask yourself, 'Will this matter one year from now? How about one month? One week? One day?'

9. Never pass up an opportunity to pee.

10. If you woke up breathing, congratulations! You have another chance!

11. Living well really is the best revenge. Being miserable because of a bad or former relationship just might mean that the other person was right about you.

12. Work is good, but it's not that important.

13. And finally, be really nice to your friends and family. You never know when you are going to need them to empty your bedpan.

❄❄❄

1. Budweiser beer conditions the hair
2. Pam cooking spray will dry finger nail polish
3. Cool whip will condition your hair in 15 min
4. Mayonnaise will KILL LICE, it will also condition your hair
5. Elmer's Glue – paint on your face, allow it to dry, peel off and see the dead skin and blackheads if any
6. Shiny Hair – use brewed Lipton Tea
7. Sunburn – empty a large jar of Nestea into your bath water
8. Minor burn – Colgate or Crest toothpaste
9. Burn your tongue? Put sugar on it!
10. Arthritis? WD-40 Spray and rub in, kill insect stings too
11. Bee stings – meat tenderizer
12. Chigger bite – Preparation H
13. Puffy eyes – Preparation H
14. Paper cut – crazy glue or chap stick (glue is used instead of sutures at most hospitals)

225

Entertaining!
Amazing!

15. Stinky feet – Jello!!
16. Athletes feet – cornstarch
17. Fungus on toenails or fingernails – Vicks vapor rub
18. Kool aid to clean dishwasher pipes. Just put in the detergent section and run a cycle, it will also clean a toilet.
19. Kool Aid can be used as a dye in paint also Kool Aid in Dannon plain yogurt as a finger paint, your kids will love it and it won't hurt them if they eat it!
20. Peanut butter – will get scratches out of CD's! Wipe off with a coffee filter paper
21. Sticking bicycle chain – Pam no-stick cooking spray
22. Pam will also remove paint, and grease from your hands! Keep a can in your garage for your hubby
23. Peanut butter will remove ink from the face of dolls.
24. When the doll clothes are hard to put on, sprinkle with cornstarch and watch them slide on
25. Heavy dandruff – pour on the vinegar!
26. Body paint – Crisco mixed with food coloring. Heat the Crisco in the microwave, pour in to an empty filcontainer and mix with the food color of your choice!
27. Tie Dye T-shirt – mix a solution of Kool Aid in a container, tie a rubber band around a section of the t-shirt and soak
28. Preserving a newspaper clipping – large bottle of club soda and cup of milk of magnesia, soak for 20 min. and let dry, will last for many years!
29. A Slinky will hold toast and CD's!
30. To keep goggles and glasses from fogging, coat with Colgate toothpaste.
31. Wine stains, pour on the Morton salt and watch it absorb into the salt.

Exciting!
Emotional!

32. To remove wax – Take a paper towel and iron it over the wax stain, it will absorb into the towel.
33. Remove labels off glassware etc. rub with peanut butter!
34. Baked on food-fill container with water, get a Bounce paper softener and the static from the Bounce towel will cause the baked on food to adhere to it. Soak overnight. Also; you can use 2 Efferdent tablets, soak overnight!
35. Crayon on the wall – Colgate toothpaste and brush it!
36. Dirty grout – Listerine
37. Stains on clothes – Colgate
38. Grass stains – Karo Syrup
39. Grease Stains – Coca Cola, it will also remove grease stains from the driveway overnight. We know it will take corrosion from batteries!
40. Fleas in your carpet? 20 Mule Team Borax – sprinkle and let stand for 24 hours. Maybe this will work if you get them back again.
41. To keep FRESH FLOWERS longer add a little Clorox, or two Bayer aspirin, or just use 7-up instead of water.
42. When you go to buy bread in the grocery store, have you ever wondered which is the freshest, so you "squeeze" for freshness or softness.? Did you know that bread is delivered fresh to the stores five days a week? Monday, Tuesday, Thursday, Friday and Saturday. Each day has a different color twist tie.

They are: Monday Blue – Tuesday Green – Thursday Red – Friday White – Saturday Yellow. So if today was Thursday, you would want red twist tie—not white which is Fridays (almost a week old)!

The colors go alphabetically by color Blue – Green – Red – White – Yellow, Monday through Saturday. Very easy to remember. I thought this was interesting. I looked in the grocery store and the bread wrappers DO have different twist ties,

227

Entertaining!
Amazing!

and even the one with the plastic clips have different colors. You learn something new everyday!!! Enjoy fresh bread when you buy bread with the right color on the day you are shopping.

❋ ❋ ❋

New Definitions:

ADULT:
A person who has stopped growing at both ends and is now growing in the middle.

BEAUTY PARLOR:
A place where women curl up and dye.

CANNIBAL:
Someone who is fed up with people.

CHICKENS:
The only animals you eat before they are born and after they are dead.

COMMITTEE:
A body that keeps minutes and wastes hours.

DUST:
Mud with the juice squeezed out.

EGOTIST:
Someone who is usually me-deep in conversation.

GOSSIP:
A person who will never tell a lie if the truth will do more damage.

Exciting!
Emotional!

Chapter 7. Hmmm...

HANDKERCHIEF:
Cold Storage.

INFLATION:
Cutting money in half without damaging the paper.

MOSQUITO:
An insect that makes you like flies better.

RAISIN:
Grape with a sunburn.

SECRET:
Something you tell to one person at a time.

SKELETON:
A bunch of bones with the person scraped off.

TOOTHACHE:
The pain that drives you to extraction.

TOMORROW:
One of the greatest labor saving devices of today.

YAWN:
An honest opinion openly expressed.

WRINKLES:
Something other people have. You have character lines.

☀ ☀ ☀

229

Entertaining!
Amazing!

Subject: Severe earthquake in France

February 14, 2003. Today it was reported that severe earthquakes have occurred in ten different locations in France. The severity was measured in excess of 10 on the Richter Scale. The cause was the 56,681 dead American soldiers buried in French soil rolling over in their graves. According to the American Battle Monuments Commission there are 26,255 Yankee dead from World War I buried in four cemeteries in France. There are 30,426 American dead from World War II buried in six cemeteries in France.

These 56,681 brave American heroes died in their youth to liberate a country which is guilty of shameful unspeakable behavior in the 21st century. May the United States of America never forget their sacrifice as we find ways to forcefully deal with the Godforsaken unappreciative, forgetful country of France!

PASS THIS AROUND! Maybe it will get to someone in France!!!

✺✺✺

Trivia Corner

All fifty states are listed across the top of the Lincoln Memorial on the back of the American $5 bill.

A cat has 32 muscles in each ear.

In 1944, records show that the army discharge papers for Major Clark Gable were signed by Capt. Ronald Reagan (the future President).

Six-year olds laugh an average of 300 times a day. Adults laugh 15 to 60 times a day.

It is impossible to lick your elbow.

A shrimp's heart is in its head.

Exciting/ Emotional!

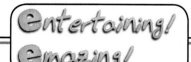

❊❊❊

A long time ago, Britain and France were at war. During one battle, the French captured an English major. Taking the major to their headquarters, the French general began to question him. The French general asked, "Why do you English officers all wear red coats? Don't you know the red material makes you easier targets for us to shoot at?" In his bland English way, the major informed the general that the reason English officers wear red coats is so that if they are shot, the blood won't show and the men they are leading won't panic. And that is why from that day to now all French Army officers wear brown pants.

❊❊❊

If your father is a poor man, it is your fate but, if your father-in-law is a poor man, it's your stupidity.

I was born intelligent: education ruined me.

A bus station is where a bus stops.
A train station is where train stops.
On my desk, I have a work station...
what more can I say...

If it's true that we are here to help others, then, what exactly are the others here for?

Since light travels faster than sound, people appear bright until you hear them speak.

231

Money is not everything.
There's MasterCard and Visa.

One should love animals.
They are so tasty.

Behind every successful man, there is a woman.
And behind every unsuccessful man, there are two.

Success is a relative term.
It brings so many relatives.

Never put off the work till tomorrow, what you can put off today.

"Your future depends on your dreams,"
So go to sleep

There should be a better way to start a day than waking up every morning.

Hard work never killed anybody, but why take the risk?

Work fascinates me. I can look at it for hours!

God made relatives.
Thank God we can choose our friends.

The more you learn, the more you know,
The more you know, the more you forget
The more you forget, the less you know
So…why learn.

☀☀☀

exciting!
emotional!

One Dollar Bill

Take out a one dollar bill. The one dollar bill you're looking at first came off the presses in 1957 in its present design.

This so-called paper money is in fact a cotton and linen blend, with red and blue minute silk fibers running through it. It is actually material. We've all washed it without it falling apart. A special blend of ink is used, the contents we will never know. It is overprinted with symbols and then it is starched to make it water resistant and pressed to give it that nice crisp look.

If you look on the front of the bill, you will see the United States Treasury Seal. On the top you will see the scales for a balanced budget. In the center you have a carpenter's square, a tool used for an even cut. Underneath is the Key to the United States Treasury. That's all pretty easy to figure out, but what is on the back of that dollar bill is something we should all know.

If you turn the bill over, you will see two circles. Both circles, together, comprise the Great Seal of the United States. The First Continental Congress requested that Benjamin Franklin and a group of men come up with a Seal. It took them four years to accomplish this task and another two years to get it approved.

If you look at the left-hand circle, you will see a Pyramid. Notice the face is lighted, and the western side is dark. This country was just beginning. We had not begun to explore the West or decided what we could do for Western Civilization. The Pyramid is un-capped, again signifying that we were not even close to being finished. Inside the capstone you have the all-seeing eye, an ancient symbol for divinity. It was Franklin's belief that one man couldn't do it alone, but a group of men, with the help of God, could do anything.

"IN GOD WE TRUST" is on this currency. The Latin above the pyramid, ANNUIT COEPTIS, means, "God has favored our undertaking."

233

Entertaining!
Amazing!

The Latin below the pyramid, NOVUS ORDO SECLORUM, means, "a new order has begun." At the base of the pyramid is the Roman Numeral for 1776. If you look at the right-hand circle, and check it carefully, you will learn that it is on every National Cemetery in the United States. It is also on the Parade of Flags Walkway at the Bushnell, Florida National Cemetery, and is the centerpiece of most heros monuments. Slightly modified, it is the seal of the President of the United States, and it is always visible whenever he speaks, yet very few people know what the symbols mean.

The Bald Eagle was selected as a symbol for victory for two reasons:

First, he is not afraid of a storm; he is strong, and he is smart enough to soar above it. Secondly, he wears no material crown. We had just broken from the King of England. Also, notice the shield is unsupported. This country can now stand on its own. At the top of that shield you have a white bar signifying congress, a unifying factor. We were coming together as one nation. In the Eagle's beak you will read, "E PLURIBUS UNUM", meaning, "one nation from many people".

Above the Eagle, you have thirteen stars, representing the thirteen original colonies, and any clouds of misunderstanding rolling away. Again, we were coming together as one.

Notice what the Eagle holds in his talons. He holds an olive branch and arrows. This country wants peace, but we will never be afraid to fight to preserve peace. The Eagle always wants to face the olive branch, but in time of war, his gaze turns toward the arrows.

They say that the number 13 is an unlucky number. This is almost a worldwide belief. You will usually never see a room numbered 13, or any hotels or motels with a 13th floor. But think about this: 13 original colonies, 13 signers of the Declaration of Independence, 13 stripes on our flag, 13 steps on the Pyramid,

Exciting!
Emotional!

13 letters in the Latin above, 13 letters in "E Pluribus Unum", 13 stars above the Eagle, 13 bars on that shield, 13 leaves on the olive branch, 13 fruits, and if you look closely, 13 arrows. And, for minorities: the 13th Amendment.

I always ask people, "Why don't you know this?" Your children don't know this, and their history teachers don't know this. Too many veterans have given up too much to ever let the meaning fade. Many veterans remember coming home to an America that didn't care. Too many veterans never came home at all.

Share this page with someone, so they can learn what is on the back of the UNITED STATES ONE DOLLAR BILL, and what it stands for...Otherwise, they will probably never know...

❋❋❋

Out To Dinner Mathematics

1. First of all, pick the number of times a week that you would like to have dinner out. (try for more than once but less than 10)

2. Multiply this number by 2 (Just to be bold)

3. Add 5. (for Sunday)

4. Multiply it by 50 – I'll wait while you get the calculator...

5. If you have already had your birthday this year add 1753...If you haven't, add 1752...

6. Now subtract the four digit year that you were born.

You should have a three digit number...

The first digit of this was your original number
(i.e., how many times you want to have eat out each week.)

235

The next two numbers are...

YOUR AGE! (Oh YES, it IS!!!!!)

THIS IS THE ONLY YEAR (2003) IT WILL EVER WORK, SO SPREAD IT AROUND WHILE IT LASTS. IMPRESSIVE, ISN'T IT?

☀☀☀

There was a case in one hospital's Intensive Care ward where patients always died in the same bed, on Sunday morning, at about 11 a.m., regardless of their medical condition. This puzzled the doctors and some even thought that it had something to do with the supernatural. No one could solve the mystery...as to why the deaths occurred around 11 a.m. on Sundays. So a World-Wide team of experts was assembled to investigate the cause of the incidents.

The next Sunday morning, a few minutes before 11 a.m., all doctors and nurses nervously wait outside the ward to see for themselves what the terrible phenomenon was all about. Some were holding wooden crosses, prayer books and other holy objects to ward off the evil spirits.

Just when the clock struck 11...Pookie Johnson, the part-time Sunday sweeper, entered the ward and unplugged the life support system so that he could use the vacuum cleaner.

☀☀☀

The average cost of rehabilitating a seal after the Exxon Valdez oil spill in Alaska was $80,000. At a special ceremony, two of the most expensively saved animals were being released back into the wild amid cheers and applause from onlookers. A minute later, in full view, a killer whale ate them both.

236

Exciting!
Emotional!

Chapter 7. Hmmm...

✹✹✹

A woman came home to find her husband in the kitchen shaking frantically, almost in a dancing frenzy, with kind of wire running from his waist towards the electric kettle. Intending to jolt him away from the deadly current, she whacked him with a handy plank of wood, breaking his arm in two places. Up to that moment, he had been happily listening to his Walkman.

✹✹✹

Two animal rights protesters were protesting at the cruelty of sending pigs to a slaughterhouse in Bonn, Germany. Suddenly, all two thousand pigs broke loose and escaped through a broken fence, stampeding madly. The two hopeless protesters were trampled to death.

✹✹✹

Iraqi terrorist Khay Rahnajet didn't pay enough postage on a letter bomb. It came back with "return to sender" stamped on it. Forgetting it was the bomb, he opened it and was blown to bits.

There now, is your day looking better?

✹✹✹

Who researches this kind of stuff?

In Lebanon, men are legally allowed to have sex with animals, but the animals must be female. Having sexual relations with a male animal is punishable by death.

(Like THAT makes sense.)

237

Entertaining!
Amazing!

In Bahrain, a male doctor may legally examine a woman's genitals, but is prohibited from looking directly at them during the examination. He may only see their reflection in a mirror.

(Do they look different reversed?)

Muslims are banned from looking at the genitals of a corpse. This also applies to undertakers; the sex organs of the deceased must be covered with a brick or piece of wood at all times.

(A brick??)

The penalty for masturbation in Indonesia is decapitation.

(I think I'd rather "go blind!")

There are men in Guam whose full-time job is to travel the countryside and deflower young virgins, who pay them for the privilege of having sex for the first time…Reason: under Guam law, it is expressly forbidden for virgins to marry.

(Let's just think for a minute; is there any job anywhere else in the world that even comes close to this?)

In Hong Kong, a betrayed wife is legally allowed to kill her adulterous husband, but may only do so with her bare hands. The husband's lover, on the other hand, may be killed in any manner desired.

(Ah! Justice!)

☀☀☀

…the best rapper is a white guy
…the best golfer is a black guy
…the Swiss hold the America's Cup

Exciting!
Emotional!

...France is accusing other countries of arrogance
...Germany doesn't want to go to war

※※※

Last month, a worldwide survey was conducted by the UN. The only question asked was:

"Would you please give your honest opinion about solutions to the food shortage in the rest of the world?"

Sadly, the survey was a huge failure...

In Africa, they didn't know what "food" meant.
In Eastern Europe, they didn't know what "honest" meant.
In Western Europe, they didn't know what "shortage" meant.
In China, they didn't know what "opinion" meant.
In the Middle East, they didn't know what "solution" meant.
In South America, they didn't know that "please" meant.
In the USA, they didn't know what "the rest of the world" meant

※※※

Passing requires 4 correct answers

1) How long did the Hundred Years War last?
2) Which country makes Panama hats?
3) From which animal do we get cat gut?
4) In which month do Russians celebrate the October Revolution?
5) What is a camel's hair brush made of?
6) The Canary Islands in the Pacific are named after what animal?

Entertaining!
Amazing!

7) What was King George VI's first name?
8) What color is a purple finch?
9) Where are Chinese gooseberries from?
All done? Check your answers on the following page!
ANSWERS TO THE QUIZ
1) How long did the Hundred Years War last?
    *116 years
2) Which country makes Panama hats?
    *Ecuador
3) From which animal do we get cat gut?
    *Sheep and Horses
4) In which month do Russians celebrate the October Revolution?
    *November
5) What is a camel's hair brush made of?
    *Squirrel fur
6) The Canary Islands in the Pacific are named after what animal?
    *Dog
7) What was King George VI's first name?
    *Albert
8) What color is a purple finch?
    *Crimson
9) Where are Chinese gooseberries from?
    *New Zealand

What do you mean you failed?
Pass this on to some other "brilliant" friends

Exciting!
Emotional!

❋❋❋

Father/Daughter Talk

A young teenage girl was about to finish her first year of college.

She considered herself to be a very liberal Democrat but her father was a rather staunch Republican.

One day she was challenging her father on his beliefs and his opposition to taxes and welfare programs. He stopped her and asked her how she was doing in school.

She answered that she had a 4.0 GPA but it was really tough. She had to study all the time, never had time to go out and party. She didn't have time for a boyfriend and didn't really have many college friends because of spending all her time studying.

He asked, "How is your friend Mary."

She replied that Mary was barely getting by. She had a 2.0 GPA, never studied, but was very popular on campus, went to all the parties all the time.

Why she often didn't show up for classes because she was hung over.

Dad then asked his daughter why she didn't go to the Dean's office and ask why she couldn't take 1.0 off her 4.0 and give it to her friend who only had a 2.0. That way they would both have a 3.0 GPA.

The daughter angrily fired back, "That wouldn't be fair, I worked really hard for mine and Mary has done nothing."

The father slowly smiled and said, "Welcome to the Republican Party."

❋❋❋

241

Entertaining!
Amazing!

This is a genuine psychological test.
It is a story about a girl.

While at the funeral of her own mother, she met this guy whom she did not know. She thought this guy was amazing, so much her dream guy she believed him to be. She fell in love with him there but never asked for his number and could not find him.

A few days later the girl killed her own sister.

Question: What is her motive in killing her sister?

Give this some thought for a while before you scroll down. Don't cheat and be as honest as possible…

Answer: She was hoping that the guy would appear at the funeral again.

If you answered this correctly, you think like a psychopath.

This was a test by a famous American psychologist used to test if one has the same mentality as a killer.

Many arrested serial killers took part in this test and answered it correctly.

If you didn't answer correctly – good for you.

If your friends hit the jackpot, may I suggest that you keep your distance.

If you got the answer correct, please let me know so I can take you off my e-mail list…

…unless that will tick you off, then I'll just be extra nice to you from now on.

❋❋❋

242

Exciting!
Emotional!

25 Signs You've Grown Up

1. Your house plants are alive, and you can't smoke any of them.
2. Having sex in a twin bed is out of the question.
3. You keep more food than beer in the fridge.
4. 6:00 AM is when you get up, not when you go to bed.
5. You hear your favorite song on an elevator.
6. You watch the Weather Channel.
7. Your friends marry and divorce instead of hook up and break up.
8. You go from 130 days of vacation time to 14.
9. Jeans and a sweater no longer qualify as "dressed up."
10. You're the one calling the police because those damn kids next door won't turn down the stereo.
11. Older relatives feel comfortable telling sex jokes around you.
12. You don't know what time Taco Bell closes anymore.
13. Your car insurance goes down and your payments go up.
14. You feed your dog Science Diet instead of McDonalds leftovers.
15. Sleeping on the couch makes your back hurt.
16. You no longer take naps from noon to 6 p.m.
17. Dinner and a movie is the whole date instead of the beginning of one.
18. Eating a basket of chicken wings at 3 a.m. would severely upset, rather than settle, your stomach.
19. You go to the drug store for ibuprofen and antacid, not condoms and pregnancy tests.
20. A $4.00 bottle of wine is no longer "pretty good stuff."
21. You actually eat breakfast food at breakfast time.

Entertaining!
Amazing!

22. "I just can't drink the way I used to," replaces, "I'm never going to drink that much again."
23. 90% of the time you spend in front of a computer is for real work.
24. You no longer drink at home to save money before going to a bar.
    And the NUMBER ONE sign that you've grown up...
25. You read this entire list looking desperately for one sign that doesn't apply to you.

☀ ☀ ☀

The following short quiz consists of four questions and tells whether you are qualified to be a "professional".

Scroll down for each answer.

The questions are not that difficult.

1. How do you put a giraffe into a refrigerator?
The correct answer is:
Open the refrigerator, put in the giraffe and close the door.
This question tests whether you tend to do simple things in an overly complicated way.

2. How do you put an elephant into a refrigerator?
Wrong Answer:
Open the refrigerator, put in the elephant and close the refrigerator.
Correct Answer:
Open the refrigerator, take out the giraffe, put in the elephant and close the door.
This tests your ability to think through the repercussions of your actions.

244

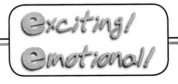

3. The Lion King is hosting an animal conference. All the animals attend except one. Which animal does not attend?

Correct Answer: The Elephant.

The Elephant is in the refrigerator.

This tests your memory.

OK, even if you did not answer the first three questions correctly, you still have one more chance to show your abilities.

4. There is a river you must cross. But it is inhabited by crocodiles. How do you manage it?

Correct Answer: You swim across. All the Crocodiles are attending the Animal Meeting.

This tests whether you learn from your mistakes.

According to Andersen Consulting Worldwide, around 90% of the professionals they tested got all questions wrong. But many pre-schoolers got several correct answers.

Andersen Consulting says this conclusively disproves the theory that most professionals have the brains of a four-year old.

Thank you for inviting MountainWings in your mailbox.

See you tomorrow.

※※※

When NASA first started sending up astronauts, they quickly discovered that ballpoint pens would not work in zero gravity. To combat the problem, NASA scientists spent a decade and $12 billion to develop a pen that writes in zero gravity,

Entertaining!
Amazing!

upside down, underwater, on almost any surface including glass and at temperatures ranging from below freezing to 300C.

The Russians used a pencil

✵✵✵

Why do full-length golf courses have 18 holes, and not 20, or 10 or an even dozen?

During a discussion among the club's membership board at St. Andrews in 1858, one of the members pointed out that it takes exactly 18 shots to polish off a fifth of Scotch. By limiting himself to only one shot of Scotch per hole, the Scot figured a round of golf was finished when the Scotch ran out.

✵✵✵

The first couple to be shown in bed together on prime time TV were Fred and Wilma Flintstone.

Every day more money is printed for Monopoly than the US Treasury.

Men can read smaller print than women can; women can hear better.

Coca-Cola was originally green.

The state with the highest percentage of people who walk to work: Alaska

The percentage of Africa that is wilderness: 28%

The percentage of North America that is wilderness: 38%

The cost of raising a medium-size dog to the age of eleven: $6,400

The average number of people airborne over the US any given hour: 61,000

Exciting!
Emotional!

Intelligent people have more zinc and copper in their hair.

The world's youngest parents were 8- and 9-years-old and lived in China in 1910.

The youngest pope was 11 years old.

The first novel ever written on a typewriter: *Tom Sawyer*.

Those San Francisco Cable cars are the only mobile National Monuments.

Each king in a deck of playing cards represents a great king from history:
Spades – King David
Hearts – Charlemagne
Clubs – Alexander, the Great
Diamonds – Julius Caesar

$111{,}111{,}111 \times 111{,}111{,}111 = 12{,}345{,}678{,}987{,}654{,}321$

If a statue in the park of a person on a horse has both front legs in the air, the person died in battle. If the horse has one front leg in the air the person died as a result of wounds received in battle. If the horse has all four legs on the ground, the person died of natural causes.

"I am." is the shortest complete sentence in the English language.

Hershey's Kisses are called that because the machine that makes them looks like it's kissing the conveyor belt.

Q. Half of all Americans live within 50 miles of what?
A. Their birthplace

Q. Most boat owners name their boats. What is the most popular boat name requested?
A. Obsession

Q. If you were to spell out numbers, how far would you have to go until you would find the letter "A"?
A. One thousand

Q. What do bulletproof vests, fire escapes, windshield wipers and laser printers all have in common?
A. All invented by women.

Q. What is the only food that doesn't spoil?
A. Honey

Q. There are more collect calls on this day than any other day of the year?
A. Father's Day

Q. What trivia fact about Mel Blanc (voice of Bugs Bunny) is the most ironic?
A. He was allergic to carrots.

Q. What is an activity performed by 40% of all people at a party?
A. Snoop in your medicine cabinet.

Exciting!
Emotional!

In Shakespeare's time, mattresses were secured on bed frames by ropes. When you pulled on the ropes the mattress tightened, making the bed firmer to sleep on. Hence the phrase "goodnight, sleep tight."

It was the accepted practice in Babylon 4,000 years ago that for a month after the wedding, the bride's father would supply his son-in-law with all the mead he could drink. Mead is a honey beer and because their calendar was lunar based, this period was called the honey month we know today as the honeymoon.

In English pubs, ale is ordered by pints and quarts. So in old England, when customers got unruly, the bartender would yell at them mind their own pints and quarts and settle down. It's where we get the phrase "mind your P's and Q's"

Many years ago in England, pub frequenters had a whistle baked into the rim or handle of their ceramic cups. When they needed a refill, they used the whistle to get some service. "Wet your whistle" is the phrase inspired by this practice.

In Scotland, a new game was invented. It was entitled Gentlemen Only Ladies Forbidden...and thus the word GOLF entered into the English language.

AND FINALLY

At least 75% of people who read this will try to lick their elbow.

✸✸✸

Entertaining!
Amazing!

Documented Screw-Ups of the year

When his 38-calibre revolver failed to fire at its intended victim during a hold-up in Long Beach, California, would be robber James Elliot did something that can only inspire wonder: He peered down the barrel and tried the trigger again. This time it worked.

The chef at a hotel in Switzerland lost a finger in a meat cutting machine and, after a little hopping around, submitted a claim to his insurance company. The company, suspecting negligence, sent out one of its men to have a look for himself. He tried the machine out and lost a finger. The chef's claim was approved.

A man who shovelled snow for an hour to clear a space for his car during a blizzard in Chicago returned with his vehicle to find a woman had taken the space. Understandably, he shot her.

After stopping for drinks at an illegal bar, a Zimbabwean bus driver found that the twenty mental patients he was supposed to be transporting from Harare to Bulawayo had escaped.

Not wanting to admit his incompetence, the driver went to a nearby bus-stop and offered everyone waiting there a free ride. He then delivered the passengers to the mental hospital, telling the staff that the patients were very excitable and prone to bizarre fantasies.

The deception wasn't discovered for three days.

An American teenager was in the hospital yesterday recovering from serious head wounds received from an oncoming train.

When asked how he received the injuries, the lad told police that he was simply trying to see how close he could get his head to a moving train before he was hit.

Exciting!
Emotional!

A mother took her daughter to the doctor and asked him to give her an examination to determine the cause of her daughters swollen abdomen.

It only took the doctor about two seconds to say "Your daughter is pregnant."

The mother turned red with fury and she argued with the doctor that her daughter was a good girl and would never compromise her reputation by having sex with a boy.

The doctor faced the window and silently watched the horizon.

The mother became enraged and screamed, "Quit looking out the window! Aren't you paying attention to me?"

"Yes, of course I am paying attention ma'am. It's just that the last time this happened, a star appeared in the East.

Every time I walk into a singles bar I can hear Mom's wise words: "Don't pick that up, you don't know where it's been."

❉❉❉

1. In many states (in the USA) the highway patrol carries two gallons of Coke in the truck to remove blood from the highway after a car accident.

2. You can put a T-bone steak in a bowl of coke and it will be gone in two days.

3. To clean a toilet: Pour a can of Coca-Cola into the toilet bowl and let the "real thing" sit for one hour, then flush clean. The citric acid in Coke removes stains from vitreous China.

4. To remove rust spots from chrome car bumpers, rub the bumper with a rumpled piece of Reynolds Wrap aluminium foil dipped in Coca Cola.

5. To clean corrosion from car battery terminals, pour a can of Coca-Cola over the terminals to bubble away the corrosion.

Entertaining!
Amazing!

6. To loosen a rusted bolt, apply a cloth soaked in Coca-Cola to the rusted bolt for several minutes.

7. To bake a moist ham, empty a can of Coca-Cola into the baking pan, wrap the ham in aluminium foil and bake. Thirty minutes before the ham is finished, remove the foil, allowing the drippings to mix with the Coke for a sumptuous brown gravy.

8. To remove grease from clothes, empty a can of Coke into a load of greasy clothes, add detergent, and run through a regular cycle. The Coca-Cola will help loosen grease stains. It will also clean road haze from your windshield.

For Your Info

1. The active ingredient in Coke is phosphoric acid. Its pH is 2.8. It will dissolve a nail in about 4 days.

2. To carry Coca-Cola syrup (the concentrate) the commercial truck must use the Hazardous material place cards reserved for highly corrosive materials.

3. The distributors of coke have been using it to clean the engines of their trucks for about 20 years!

☀ ☀ ☀

Zen thoughts for those who take life too seriously.

* A day without sunshine is like, night.
* On the other hand, you have different fingers.
* I feel like I'm diagonally parked in a parallel universe.
* Honk if you love peace and quiet.
* He who laughs last thinks slowest.
* I drive way too fast to worry about cholesterol.
* Support bacteria. They're the only culture some people have.
* A clear conscience is usually the sign of a bad memory.

Exciting!
Emotional!

* OK, so what's the speed of dark?
* Hard work pays off in the future. Laziness pays off now.
* Everyone has a photographic memory. Some just don't have film.
* Eagles may soar, but weasels don't get sucked into jet engines.
* What happens if you get scared half to death twice?

And my personal favorite…

* Inside every older person is a younger person wondering what the hell happened.

✺✺✺

The Bingo Card

This guy had a very attractive wife, who was always wanting clothes, jewelry, etc., but he was not too well off. One day his wife came home with a diamond necklace.

The guy asked: "Where did you get that?"

His wife replied: "I won it at bingo."

The next night she came home with a mink coat.

The guy asked: "Where did you get that?"

His wife replied: "I won it at bingo."

The next night she came home with a Mercedes Benz.

The husband asked: "Where did you get that?"

His wife replied: "Look!! Don't keep asking where I get my things!! Go upstairs and run my bath for me!!"

His wife came upstairs to find a small amount of water in the tub.

The wife asked: "How come you put so little water in the tub?"

The guy replied: "I didn't want you to get your bingo card wet!"

Entertaining!
Amazing!

World's Funniest and Greatest E-mails

Old Age

Two elderly gentlemen from a retirement center were sitting on a bench under a tree when one turns to the other and says, "Slim, I'm 73 years old now and I'm just full of aches and pains. I know you're about my age. How do you feel?"

Slim says, "Hell, I feel just like a new-born baby."

"Really? Like a baby?"

"Yep. No hair, no teeth, and I think I just shit my pants.

❋❋❋

Subject: Some things we keep!

I grew up in the fifties with practical parents – a mother, God love her, who washed aluminum foil after she cooked in it, then reused it. She was the original recycle queen, before they had a name for it...

A father who was happier getting old shoes fixed than buying new ones.

Their marriage was good, their dreams focused.

Their best friends lived barely a wave away. I can see them now, Dad in trousers, tee shirt and a hat and Mom in a house dress, lawn mower in one hand, dishtowel in the other.

It was the time for fixing things – a curtain rod, the kitchen radio, screen door, the oven door, the hem in a dress. Things we keep.

It was a way of life, and sometimes it made me crazy.

All that re-fixing, reheating, renewing, I wanted just once to be wasteful.

Waste meant affluence. Throwing things away meant there'd always be more.

But then my Mother died, and on that clear summer's night, in the warmth of the hospital room, I was struck with the pain of learning that sometimes there isn't any 'more.'

254

Sometimes, what we care about most gets all used up and goes away...never to return.

So...while we have it...it's best we love it...and care for it...and fix it when it's broken...and heal it when it's sick.

This is true...for marriage...and old cars...and children with bad report cards...and dogs with bad hips...and aging parents...and grandparents.

We keep them because they are worth it, because we are worth it.

Some things we keep.

Like a best friend that moved away – or – a classmate we grew up with. There are just some things that make life important, like people we know who are special...and so, we keep them close!

Now send this to all those people that are "keepers" in your life...like you!!

✸✸✸

Confusing Signs

Sign seen on a bathroom door: TOILET DOES NOT WORK, PLEASE USE FLOOR BELOW.

Sign in Laundromat: Automatic Washing Machines: PLEASE REMOVE ALL YOUR CLOTHES WHEN THE LIGHT GOES OUT.

In a London Department store: BARGAIN BASEMENT UPSTAIRS.

Sign in an office: WOULD THE PERSON WHO TOOK THE STEP LADDER YESTERDAY PLEASE BRING IT BACK, OR FURTHER STEPS WILL BE TAKEN.

In an office: AFTER TEA BREAK, STAFF SHOULD EMPTY THE TEAPOT AND STAND UPSIDE DOWN ON THE DRAIN BOARD.

Outside a thrift shop: WE EXCHANGE ANYTHING – BICYCLES, WASHING MACHINES, BRING YOUR WIFE ALONG, AND GET A WONDERFUL BARGAIN!

Notice in health food shop window: CLOSED DUE TO ILLNESS

Spotted in a safari park: ELEPHANTS PLEASE STAY IN YOUR CAR

Seen during a conference: FOR ANYONE WHO HAS CHILDREN AND DOESN'T KNOW IT, THERE'S A DAY CARE CENTER ON THE FIRST FLOOR.

Seen in a field: THE FARMER ALLOWS WALKERS TO CROSS THE FIELD FOR FREE, BUT THE BULL CHARGES.

Message on a leaflet: IF YOU CANNOT READ, THIS LEAFLET WILL TELL YOU HOW TO GET LESSONS.

On a repair shop store window: WE CAN REPAIR ANYTHING.
(PLEASE KNOCK HARD ON THE DOOR, BELL DOES NOT WORK)

※ ※ ※

Something To Think About

Joe Smith started the day early having set his alarm clock (MADE IN JAPAN) for 6:00 a.m. While his coffeepot (MADE IN CHINA) was perking, he shaved with his electric razor (MADE IN HONG KONG). He put on a dress shirt (MADE IN SRI LANKA), designer jeans (MADE IN SINGAPORE) and tennis shoes (MADE IN KOREA). After cooking his breakfast in his new electric skillet (MADE IN INDIA) he sat down with his calculator (MADE IN MEXICO) to see how much he could spend today. After setting his watch (MADE IN TAIWAN) to the radio (MADE IN INDIA) he got in his car (MADE IN GERMANY) and continued his search for a

good paying A M E R I C A N   J O B. At the end of yet another discouraging and
fruitless day, Joe decided to relax for a while. He put on his sandals (MADE IN
BRAZIL) poured himself a glass of wine (MADE IN FRANCE) and turned on his
TV (MADE IN INDONESIA), and then wondered why he can't find a good paying
job in A M E R I C A...

❀❀❀

(Iowa) Several years ago, an adventurous pair decided to take their ropes and
rappel off the Boone Scenic Valley Railroad train over the Des Moines river.
Words can't describe how breathtakingly high this narrow train bridge is over the
river valley. The open train ride over the abyss is both stunningly beautiful and
somewhat nerve-wracking.

Our adventurers had to be completely fearless, because they walked to the
middle of this narrow railroad bridge, tied off their ropes, and began to rappel
down. When the train came by on it's daily tour of the valley, their one mistake
became apparent. They had tied the ropes to the sturdiest support possible: the
steel train tracks...

DARWIN AWARD: What's That Sound?

2 August 2002, Kansas: Police said an Olathe man was struck and killed by a
train after his vehicle broke down on Interstate 35. His attempts at repairing his
car had failed, and he was calling for help when the train engineer spotted him
standing on the tracks. The engineer said the man was holding a cell phone to one
ear, and cupping his hand to the other ear to block the noise of the train.

Entertaining!
Amazing!

DARWIN AWARD: A Rocky Roll

Confirmed True

29 August 2002, Washington: An innovative petty crime spree turned into a Darwinian opportunity when a Vancouver man fell out of a minivan while throwing rocks.

Five men had been denting mailboxes and moving cars with their low-tech missiles, when 23-year-old John decided he needed a wider range of targets. As the Ford Aerostar cruised through a residential neighborhood, he left his compatriots at the windows while he opened the sliding door. One mighty throw later, he pitched through the opening, struck his head on the pavement, and suffered the ultimate penalty for his crime: stone cold death.

PERSONAL ACCOUNT: Lion Lunch

2002: As a Ranger, I am inured to the stupidity of the public when confronted with wild animals, but my daughter's experience in South Africa takes the cake. She worked in the Kruger National Park, where park authorities are scrupulous about warning people to remain within their cars at all times. A tourist driving through the park was motivated to ignore the rules when she spotted a lioness and her cubs. The woman's husband recalls her saying the cubs were not posed correctly, so she nipped out of the car and picked one up to move it closer to its siblings.

Needless to say, the lioness shared her with the cubs.

✸✸✸

Exciting!
Emotional!

How To Keep A Healthy Level of Insanity

1. At lunch time, sit in your parked car with sunglasses on and point a hair dryer at passing cars. See if they slow down.

2. Page yourself over the intercom. Don't disguise your voice.

3. Every time someone asks you to do something, ask if they want fries with that.

4. Put your garbage can on your desk and label it "in".

5. Put decaf in the coffee maker for three weeks. Once everyone has gotten over their caffeine addictions, switch to espresso.

6. In the memo field of all your checks, write "for sexual favors."

7. Finish all your sentences with "in accordance with the prophecy."

8. Don't use any punctuation marks.

9. As often as possible, skip rather than walk.

10. Ask people what sex they are. Laugh hysterically after they answer.

11. Specify that your drive-through order is "to go".

12. Sing along at the opera.

13. Go to a poetry recital and ask why the poems don't rhyme.

14. Put mosquito netting around your work area. Play a tape of jungle sounds all day.

15. Five days in advance, tell your friends you can't attend their party because you're not in the mood.

16. Have your co-workers address you by your wrestling name, Rock Hard Kim.

17. When the money comes out the ATM, scream "I won!", "I won!" "Third time this week!!!!!"

18. When leaving the zoo, start running towards the parking lot, yelling, "run for your lives, they're loose!!"

Entertaining!
Amazing!

19. Tell your children over dinner, "due to the economy, we are going to have to let one of you go."

✺✺✺

The Stella's are named after 81-year-old Stella Liebeck who spilled coffee on herself and successfully sued McDonalds. That case inspired the Stella Awards for the most frivolous successful lawsuits in the United States.

The following are this year's candidates:

1. Kathleen Robertson of Austin, Texas, was awarded $780,000 by a jury of her peers after breaking her ankle tripping over a toddler who was running inside a furniture store. The owners of the store were understandably surprised at the verdict, considering the misbehaving little toddler was Ms. Robertson's son.

2. A 19-year-old Carl Truman of Los Angeles won $74,000 and medical expenses when his neighbor ran over his hand with a Honda Accord. Mr. Truman apparently didn't notice there was someone at the wheel of the car when he was trying to steal his neighbor's hub caps.

3. Terrence Dickson of Bristol, Pennsylvania, was leaving a house he had just finished robbing by way of the garage. He was not able to get the garage door to go up since the automatic door opener was malfunctioning. He couldn't re-enter the house because the door connecting the house and garage locked when he pulled it shut. The family was on vacation, and Mr. Dickson found himself locked in the garage for eight days. He subsisted on a case of Pepsi he found, and a large bag of dry dog food. He sued the homeowner's insurance claiming the situation caused him undue mental anguish. The jury agreed to the tune of $500.000.

Chapter 7. Hmmm...

4. Jerry Williams of Little Rock, Arkansas, was awarded $14,500 and medical expenses after being bitten on the buttocks by his next door neighbor's beagle. The beagle was on a chain in its owner's fenced yard. The award was less than sought because the jury felt the dog might have been just a little provoked at the time by Mr. Williams, who was shooting it repeatedly with a pellet gun.

5. A Philadelphia restaurant was ordered to pay Amber Carson of Lancaster, Pennsylvania, $113,500 after she slipped on a soft drink and broke her coccyx (tailbone). The beverage was on the floor because Ms. Carson had thrown it at her boyfriend 30 seconds earlier during an argument.

6. Kara Walton of Claymont, Delaware, successfully sued the owner of a night club in a neighboring city when she fell from the bathroom window to the floor and knocked out her two front teeth. This occurred while Ms. Walton was trying to sneak through the window in the ladies room to avoid paying the $3.50 cover charge. She was awarded $12,000 and dental expenses.

7. This year's favorite could easily be Mr. Merv Grazinski of Oklahoma City, Oklahoma. Mr. Grazinski purchased a brand new 32-foot Winnebago motor home. On his first trip home, having driven onto the freeway, he set the cruise control at 70 mph and calmly left the drivers seat to go into the back and make himself a cup of coffee. Not surprisingly, the R.V. left the freeway, crashed and overturned. Mr. Grazinski sued Winnebago for not advising him in the owner's manual that he couldn't actually do this. The jury awarded him $1,750,000 plus a new motor home. The company actually changed their manuals on the basis of this suit, just in case there were any other complete morons buying their recreation vehicles.

261

Entertaining!
Amazing!

※ ※ ※

A physician claims these are actual comments from his patients made while he was performing colonoscopies:

1. "Take it easy, Doc, you're boldly going where no man has gone before."
2. "Find Amelia Earhart yet?"
3. "Can you hear me NOW?"
4. "Oh boy, that was sphincterrific!"
5. "Are we there yet? Are we there yet? Are we there yet?"
6. "You know, in Arkansas, we're now legally married."
7. "Any sign of the trapped miners, Chief?"
8. "You put your left hand in, you take your left hand out.
   You do the Hokey Pokey…"
9. "Hey! Now I know how a Muppet feels!"
10. "If your hand doesn't fit, then you must quit!"
11. "Hey, Doc, let me know if you find my dignity."
12. "You used to be an executive at Enron, didn't you?"
13. "Could you write me a note for my wife, saying that my head is
    not in fact, up there?"

※ ※ ※

Just in case you weren't feeling old enough today, this will certainly change things.

The people who are starting college this fall across the nation were born in 1983. They have no idea when or why Jordache jeans were cool.

262

Popcorn has always been cooked in the microwave.

They have never seen Larry Bird play.

They never took a swim and thought about Jaws.

Bottle caps have always been screw off and plastic.

They don't know who Mork was or where he was from.

(The correct answer, by the way, is Ork)

They never heard: "Where's the beef?", "I'd walk a mile for a Camel," or "De plane, de plane!"

They do not care who shot J.R. and have no idea who J.R. was.

Kansas, Chicago, Boston, America, and Alabama are places, not bands.

There has always been MTV.

The statement "You sound like a broken record" means nothing to them.

They have never owned a record player.

They have likely never played Pac Man and have never heard of Pong.

The Compact Disc was introduced when they were 1 year old.

They have always had an answering machine.

Most have never seen a TV set with only 13 channels, nor have they seen a black and white TV.

They have always had cable.

There have always been VCRs, but they have no idea what BETA was.

They cannot fathom not having a remote control.

They don't know about the "Help me, I've fallen and I can't get up" commercial.

They were born the year that Walkmen were introduced by Sony.

Roller-skating has always meant inline for them.

Michael Jackson has always been white.

They can't imagine what hard contact lenses are.

263

Entertaining!
Amazing!

They are too young to remember the space shuttle blowing up.
They don't have a clue how to use a typewriter.

❊ ❊ ❊

A government which robs Peter to pay Paul can always depend on the support of Paul. —George Bernard Shaw

A liberal is someone who feels a great debt to his fellow man, which debt he proposes to pay off with your money. —G. Gordon Liddy

Democracy must be something more than two wolves and a sheep voting on what to have for dinner. —James Bovard (1994)

Foreign aid might be defined as a transfer from poor people in rich countries to rich people in poor countries. —Douglas Casey (1992)

Giving money and power to government is like giving whiskey and car keys to teenage boys. —P.J. O'Rourke

Government's view of the economy could be summed up in a few short phrases: If it moves, tax it. If it keeps moving, regulate it. And if it stops moving, subsidize it. —Ronald Reagan (1986)

I don't make jokes. I just watch the government and report the facts. —Will Rogers

If you think health care is expensive now, wait until you see what it costs when it's free. —P.J. O'Rourke

264

Exciting!
Emotional!

If you want government to intervene domestically, you're a liberal.
If you want government to intervene overseas, you're a conservative.
If you want government to intervene everywhere, you're a moderate.
If you don't want government to intervene anywhere, you're an extremist.
—Joseph Sobran (1995)

No man's life, liberty, or property are safe while the legislature is in session.
—Mark Twain (1866)

Suppose you were an idiot. And suppose you were a member of Congress. But I repeat myself. —Mark Twain

The government is like a baby's alimentary canal, with a happy appetite at one end and no responsibility at the other. —Ronald Reagan

The inherent vice of capitalism is the unequal sharing of the blessings. The inherent blessing of socialism is the equal sharing of misery. —Winston Churchill

The only difference between a tax man and a taxidermist is that the taxidermist leaves the skin. —Mark Twain

The ultimate result of shielding men from the effects of folly is to fill the world with fools. —Herbert Spencer (1891)

There is no distinctly native American criminal class save Congress. —Mark Twain

What this country needs are more unemployed politicians. —Edward Langley

When buying and selling are controlled by legislation, the first things to be bought and sold are legislators. —P.J. P'Rourke

Entertaining!
Emazing!

※※※

1. Never, under any circumstances, take a sleeping pill and a laxative on the same night.

2. If you had to identify, in one word, the reason why the human race has not achieved, and never will achieve, its full potential, that word would be "meetings."

3. There is a very fine line between "hobby" and "mental illness."

4. People who want to share their religious views with you almost never want you to share yours with them.

5. And when God, who created the entire universe with all of its glories, decides to deliver a message to humanity, He WILL NOT use, as His messenger, a person on cable TV with a bad hairstyle.

6. You should not confuse your career with your life.

7. No matter what happens, somebody will find a way to take it too seriously.

8. When trouble arises and things look bad, there is always one individual who perceives a solution and is willing to take command. Very often, that individual is crazy.

9. Nobody cares if you can't dance well. Just get up and dance.

10. Never lick a steak knife.

11. Take out the fortune before you eat the cookie.

12. The most destructive force in the universe is gossip.

13. You will never find anybody who can give you a clear and compelling reason why we observe daylight savings time.

14. You should never say anything to a woman that even remotely suggests that you think she's pregnant unless you can see an actual baby emerging from her at that moment.

266

Exciting!
Emotional!

15. There comes a time when you should stop expecting other people to make a big deal about your birthday. That time is age eleven.

16. The one thing that unites all human beings, regardless of age, gender, religion, economic status or ethnic background, is that, deep down inside, we ALL believe that we are above average drivers.

17. The main accomplishment of almost all organized protests is to annoy people who are not in them.

18. A person who is nice to you, but rude to the waiter, is not a nice person. (This is very important. Pay attention. It never fails.)

19. Respect the idiots around you. They make you look so much better.

20. Your friends love you anyway.

✳✳✳

The most destructive habit...Worry
The greatest Joy...Giving
The greatest loss...Loss of self-respect
The most satisfying work...Helping others
The ugliest personality trait...Selfishness
The most endangered species...Dedicated leaders
Our greatest natural resource...Our youth
The greatest "shot in the arm"...Encouragement
The greatest problem to overcome...Fear
The most effective sleeping pill...Peace of mind
The most crippling failure disease...Excuses
The most powerful force in life...Love
The most dangerous pariah...A gossiper

267

Entertaining!
Amazing!

World's Funniest and Greatest E-mails

The world's most incredible computer...The brain
The worst thing to be without...Hope
The deadliest weapon...The tongue
The two most power-filled words..."I Can"
The greatest asset...Faith
The most worthless emotion...Self-pity
The most beautiful attire...SMILE!
The most prized possession...Integrity
The most powerful channel of communication...Prayer
The most contagious spirit...Enthusiasm
The most important thing in life...GOD

Everyone needs this list to live by.

Exciting!
Emotional!

LaVergne, TN USA
25 March 2011
221682LV00005B/34/P